Friendship
as a
Social
Institution

Friendship
as a
Social
Institution

George J. McCall,
Michal M. McCall,
Norman K. Denzin,
Gerald D. Suttles,
and Suzanne B. Kurth

ALDINETRANSACTION
A Division of Transaction Publishers
New Brunswick (U.S.A.) and London (U.K.)

First paperback edition 2011
Copyright © 1970 by Transaction Publishers, New Brunswick, New Jersey.

All rights reserved under International and Pan-American Copyright Conventions. No part of this book may be reproduced or transmitted in any form or by any means, electronic or mechanical, including photocopy, recording, or any information storage and retrieval system, without prior permission in writing from the publisher. All inquiries should be addressed to AldineTransaction, A Division of Transaction Publishers, Rutgers—The State University of New Jersey, 35 Berrue Circle, Piscataway, New Jersey 08854-8042. www.transactionpub.com

This book is printed on acid-free paper that meets the American National Standard for Permanence of Paper for Printed Library Materials.

Library of Congress Catalog Number: 2010024458
ISBN: 978-0-202-36355-4
Printed in the United States of America

Library of Congress Cataloging-in-Publication Data

Friendship as a social institution / George J. McCall ... [et al.].
        p. cm.
    Originally published under title: Social relationships, Chicago : Aldine Pub. Co., [1970].
    Includes bibliographical references and index.
    ISBN 978-0-202-36355-4 (alk. paper)
        1. Interpersonal relations. I. McCall, George J.

HM132.S57 2010
302.3'4--dc22

                                                    2010024458

Contents

Preface

The analysis of social relationships is among the many neglected problems in modern sociology. Although the special importance of dyadic relationships between individuals was remarked on by the pioneer figures in sociology, and although social relationships are a numerous and widely prevalent species of social organization, they have generally received short shrift since at least the beginning of World War II. The reign of macrosociologists has contributed to this neglect, of course, and sociologists interested in interpersonal phenomena have been more interested in small groups and interactive encounters than in social relationships. What dyadic analyses we have had in modern times tend to focus on role relationships rather than social relationships.

Nevertheless, there remains an interest in social relationships as proved by an occasional article and recurrent sessions at professional meetings, as well as by the layman's personal concern with his own "relationships."

Papers of generalizing theoretical import on social relationships are particularly uncommon. Consequently, when I chanced to encounter the five essays that constitute the core of this volume and discovered the unusually clear theoretical links among them, I felt they would profit from common publication.

The independent preparation of these papers needs to be properly emphasized. Although all five authors have been associated with the Urbana campus of the University of Illinois during the 1960's, and although some of us had known each other, none of us had discussed our respective ideas on social relationships with another. The close theoretical affinities of these papers stems entirely from our common exposure to the symbolic interactionist tradition.

To explore the mutual relevance of our respective ideas, a conference was held at the Chicago Circle campus. It was decided there that our five papers should be published in their virtually original form to preserve this independence of thought and that our collective discussion of social relationships be confined to a collaborative final chapter in an "overview." To guide the reader toward this collective overview, brief editorial introductions have been added to the essays to provide continuity, tacitly explicating the rationale for the order of presentation.

G.J.M.

Contributors

George J. McCall is Professor of Sociology at the University of Illinois, Chicago Circle Campus

Michal M. McCall was formerly an Instructor of Sociology at the University of Illinois, Chicago Circle Campus

Norman K. Denzin is Assistant Professor of Sociology at the University of California, Berkeley

Gerald D. Suttles is Associate Professor of Sociology at the University of Chicago

Suzanne B. Kurth is Assistant Professor of Sociology at the University of Tennessee

Social Relationships

The Social Organization
of Relationships

The initial essay in this volume is broader in scope than those that follow, providing a programmatic framework for the analysis of social relationships as social organizations. It describes the nature of social relationships and differentiates it from similar phenomena, such as interactive encounters, groups, and role relationships. Having defined the concept of social relationships, the essay examines certain organizational features of relationships—their substance, shape, structure, and culture—and the distinctive forms these features assume in this smallest of enduring social organizations. The life of social relationships is viewed in terms both of organizational dynamics (such as recruitment, socialization, interaction, innovation, social control, and logistics) and of organizational change.

I am grateful to Michal M. McCall and to J. L. Simmons for many fruitful discussions of social relationships, which did much to give form to the ideas expressed here.

Social relationships have received little explicit attention in modern sociology. In the first twenty-five volumes of the *American Sociological Review*, not a single article has been indexed as dealing with social relationships (*Index*, 1961). In the first seventy volumes of the *American Journal of Sociology*, only six articles have been so indexed, mostly inaccurately (*Cumulative Index*, 1966).

One reason for this general neglect of dyadic relationships, I propose, is that after the early triumphs of Cooley (1902, 1909), Simmel (1950), Weber (1947), and Waller (1938), the rise to fashion of imported frameworks diverted those sociologists interested in interpersonal phenomena from their concern with social organization. One such diversion was *role theory,* an essentially culturological approach borrowed from anthropolgy (Nadel, 1957; Parsons, 1951). Role theory changed the focus from the relations among persons to relations among social roles as abstract patterns of expectations, rights, and duties. A second imported framework was *interpersonal theory,* as presented by Sullivan, Freud, and others (Sullivan, 1964; Mullahy, 1949). Emphasis was placed upon the interplay of psychic dynamics and displaced from the manifold external relations among social actors. A more recent diversion has been *balance theory* as developed by such social psychologists as Heider (1958), Newcomb (1953), and Cartwright (1956). Balance theory focused on certain relations among people's attitudes toward one another and toward relevant common objects.

We have learned much from each of these approaches, as I shall show below, but none of them takes aim at the core sociological characteristic of social relationships—namely, that they are a form of social organization, comparable in many respects to small groups, bureaucracies, or communities. It is this aspect that I wish to explore in the present paper.

Following Max Weber (1947, pp. 118–20), a relationship is at base the existence of a substantial probability of interaction between two persons. What makes such a relationship social is the *basis* for the existence of this probability of interaction and the *form* the interaction will likely assume. In social relationships the basis for the probability of interaction is that the two persons view themselves as the sole members of a common collectivity—e.g., a marriage—constraining them both to interact in a more or less specific fashion.

At one extreme this common collectivity may be a role relationship. If a person wanders off the street into an ice cream parlor, he will not long ignore the woman behind the counter nor will he lick her nose; he will probably ask about or request some dairy product. Similarly, she will not long ignore him nor will she flick peanut shells in his hair; she will probably ask him if she can be of assistance to him with regard to dairy products. That is, each of them perceives himself and the other to be the members of a particular role relationship (clerk–customer) and feels constrained to interact with the other in a manner befitting their common membership in this collectivity. The social relationship is between the two persons, however, *not* between the two roles; the role relationship only constrains the form the interaction takes. Where such a role relationship is the primary constraint on the form of interaction, we can speak of a *formal relationship* between two persons.

At the other extreme, the common collectivity of which they are members may be merely an acquaintanceship—the existence of mutual recognition. That is to say, two persons feel constrained to interact in at least some minimal fashion, as by waving or saying hello, simply because each recognizes the other as a distinctive individual and knows that the other recognizes him. Perception of themselves as members of even such a contentless collectivity is sufficient to constrain them to interact, and the form this interaction takes is constrained by what one knows of other and by what one thinks or hopes the other knows of him. Where knowledge of persons rather than role relationships is the primary constraint on the form of interaction, we can speak of a *personal relationship* between two persons (McCall and Simmons, 1966, p. 169).

Virtually all concrete social relationships are, of course, blends of formal and personal relationships. Even where a role relationship is the major constraint on interaction, the actors know a good deal about one another (such as age, sex, class, beauty, etc.) and take this knowledge into account in forming their respective lines of action. Similarly, personal relationships almost always involve knowledge and assumption of role relationships between the members (e.g., those of age peers or friends) (Hughes, 1945; Strauss, 1959, pp. 69–76; McCall and Simmons, 1966, pp. 130–46).

If the views expressed above are correct, then the variations and vicissitudes of social relationships must be approached by considering the organization, dynamics, and changes of dyadic collectivities constraining their members. We turn now to each of these aspects successively.

Organizational Components of Relationships

In treating the social organization of a relationship, we will examine its substance (the bonds uniting the persons in a relationship), its structure (or shape), and its culture.

BONDS

If a social relationship is to be viewed as a form of social organization, the participants or members must be bound together into some unit larger than themselves. Analysis of such binding forces reveals at least five types of social bonds (McCall and Simmons, 1966, pp. 170–75).

First, there is in many relationships an element of *ascription.* That is, owing simply to the social positions two persons happen to occupy, and quite independent of any individual characteristics, these persons may be linked by a role relationship. The prototypical case is of course those social relationships based upon blood relation or kinship, as described by anthropologists. In modern societies the force of kinship has become attenuated, but even here individuals inherit many social ties and have many others foisted upon them by their social groupings. For example, many teacher–pupil, supervisor–employee, and colleague or peer relationships are, in this fashion, ascribed.

In addition to these passive forms of ascription, people actively strive to achieve many social "ascriptions." They seek to have their relationships legitimated and consecrated by being conferred upon themselves and alter by officials of their social groupings. Many social positions thus "ascribed"—a doctorate, a licensed occupation, a military rank—exist and are largely defined in terms of specifying the ascriptive component of a whole set of relationships to other positions.

Second, there is in many if not most social relationships the factor of *commitment*. To a varying extent a person has privately and publicly committed himself, or been committed, to honoring a restrictive covenant, a trade agreement, with the other party. He has pledged the semi-exclusive use of the other party as a source of certain specified behaviors, role supports, and other rewards. He has committed himself to the legitimation of certain aspects of certain *role-identities*[1] by endorsing the other party as a partner in enacting them and as an audience whose opinions about his performances of these identities are given primary weight.

Commitments are a strategy for increasing and insuring the dependability of a source of exchange rewards (Becker, 1960). But they are much more. They are frequently entered into because of moral convictions, as well as, or even instead of, opportunism or desire. If in a relationship there are no elements except commitment based upon moral convictions, the relationship is literally only a duty. Even if the commitment is not *made* on moral grounds, the person is under some moral obligation to fulfill it. To have made a commitment is to have bound oneself, and it requires a very good excuse to withdraw from alter without losing face. Even personal relationships are thus at least partly public affairs.

Although ascriptions and commitments often blend, we must be careful to distinguish between them. Persons often enter into what they think are commitments (e.g., going steady) only to discover later that they have effectively recruited themselves into "ascribed" relationships they cannot dissolve without the formal consent of their social groupings (e.g., marriage).

Third, the members of a relationship may be bound by the factor of *attachment*. Attachments to others are formed as the individual's identities evolve and change. One's dreams of oneself, the idealized pictures he has of himself in certain social positions, are seldom constant over long periods of time. As a person faces new tasks and new alters, these tasks and alters become incorpo-

---

1. A role-identity is a person's imaginative view of himself as he likes to think of himself being and acting as an occupant of a particular social position (McCall and Simmons, 1966, pp. 63–76).

rated into his daydreaming about himself in these social roles. Consequently, *specific persons and their behaviors get built into the contents of role-identities* and become crucial to the legitimation and enactment of these identities. This building of specific others into the very contents of role-identities is what we mean by becoming "attached" to particular alters.

Such attachments make the individual vulnerable to the decisions, reactions, and whims of these others and to all the physical and social vicissitudes that may befall them. As the Buddhists put it, to become involved with another is to surrender a hostage to the fates. When one becomes attached to a particular other, the resulting relationship tends to become "nontransferable." Any competent clerk or repairman will do, but one cannot so easily go looking for another mother, another brother, another child. The less transferable a relationship, the more vulnerable the members are.

Fourth, *investment* is a ubiquitous and powerful bond between persons. When someone has expended such scarce resources as money, time, and life chances in establishing and maintaining a relationship, he cannot afford to throw them away without realizing substantial returns. The normative standards involved in most relationships—sometimes termed the "norm of reciprocity" (Gouldner, 1960)—demand that we also show some consideration for alter's investments as well, for the tie is, after all, a joint venture.

Fifth, *reward dependability* is a major reason for the existence and continuation of many relationships. As a consequence of our recurring needs for role-support and the other commodities of social exchange, we are disposed to seek dependably recurring *sources* of them. And when we locate or are thrown together with individuals or groups that for whatever reason are able, willing, and ready to afford us supplies of such exchange commodities, we are disposed to seek to "corner the market" by establishing further and more durable bonds with those alters—bonds of ascription, commitment, attachment, and investment.

These five bonds are, then, perhaps the most important forces serving to bind two persons together, making it likely that they will continue to interact on a personal basis in the future. Ascrip-

tion, commitment, attachment, investment, and reward dependability are the social psychological glue that cements individuals
into the units we know as social relationships.

These bonds usually blend and run together in most continuing
relationships. Nevertheless they are distinct factors; they are
present in different proportions in different relationships, and
they often vary independently of one another. For example, we
sometimes have commitments that differ from those ascribed to
us; we frequently forgo the potential rewards of exchanges because of "prior commitments"; we fret over interpersonal investments that have not yet yielded dependable reward sources; we
seek to secure our attachments through mutual commitments and
formal ascriptions; and conversely, we may resignedly fulfill
commitments that no longer reflect our attachments.

Individuals are most preoccupied with their attachments, but
the societies they live in are most concerned with their ascriptions
and commitments. At the least, social forces seek to produce in
the individual a set of commitments that correspond to and im-
plement his ascriptions. If ascriptions, commitments, and attachments are all aligned, conventional social opinion regards this
consistency as even better. But the person is not simply left on
his honor in these matters. Such ascriptions and commitments,
once made, are enforced by a host of informal social pressures
and formal social controls, and ordinarily the individual cannot
seriously violate them without incurring retribution.

A wide divergence between one's commitments and one's attachments is likely to engender a good deal of personal discontent,
and the person will be motivated to reduce the divergence, either
by giving up his attachments or by changing his commitments—
his job, his spouse, his style of life. But neither of these strategies
is easily brought off, and most of us carry around some freight of
discontent and restlessness because the two sets of factors are not
mutually aligned. Most frequently we attempt compromise solutions of moderate divergences by negotiating redefinitions of the
contents of the commitments and by reshuffling the intensities
of our attachments.

People tend to make investments on the basis of their attachments, particularly in the early phases of relationships, in attempts

to secure commitments from the other parties as dependable sources of exchange rewards. In later phases, however, a person must often continue to invest in the relationship even though his attachments may have shifted to some extent or even though alter proves somewhat unreliable as a source of reward. His resources are quite limited, as we have seen, and hence he cannot afford simply to throw away what he has already "put into" the relationship and start anew. This dilemma is, in fact, particularly common in many of the deepest and most intimate associations, like marriage, parenthood, and career ties. After a certain point, many such investments are virtually irreversible.

STRUCTURE

Having briefly examined some bases for the likelihood of continuing interaction between two persons—some bonds that unite people in a social relationship—we turn to a consideration of the shape and structure of such relationships.

Shape is perhaps more easily defined in relatively *formal* relationships, where we may conceive of it as the fit between a pair (or more likely several pairs) of social roles, such as district attorney and judge, that serve as the primary constraints on the form of interaction between the two persons. There are several points in the definition. First, we are talking about *social* roles, sets of expectations commonly held concerning the conduct, rights, and duties of any occupant of specified social positions. As such, social roles are essentially cultural objects of which individuals may have learned more or less. Second, the fit between such social roles is a matter of *functional* fit—the manner in which the expected conduct, rights, and duties of one social position facilitate or impede those of the other position. Third, such a fit between social roles constrains the form of interaction between two persons only insofar as the social situation or the limits of their knowledge of one another makes this pair of social positions the most salient guide to shaping their lines of conduct toward one another.

All this may seem to be a laborious way to say that the shape of a formal relationship is roughly bounded by the role relationship(s) between the members' social positions as outlined (rather sketchily) by the prevailing local culture. And so it may be, but I have spelled it out in this fashion in the hope that it might, one, remind the reader that the role relationship is not identical with the formal relationship but only bounds its structure, and, two, might facilitate definition of the personal relationship.

It is here assumed that the self-structure of each individual is a complexly organized set of *role-identities*—conceptions of himself as an occupant of a number of social positions, conceptions not perfectly or equally compatible. It is further assumed that no other person is acquainted with the entire set either of social positions or of role-identities and that for reasons of economy and security the individual reveals somewhat different subsets of these positions and/or role-identities to different alters. I will refer to any one of these revealed subsets of identities as a *persona* presented by that individual (McCall and Simmons, 1966, pp. 76–94, 181–83).

With these preliminaries, we may define the shape of a *personal* relationship as the fit between the *personas* that the members of a relationship present to one another. Again, several points must be noted. First, although social positions and social roles are again involved, the self-conceptions are the critical elements here. That is, the conventional roles are idiosyncratically adapted and reworked by the individual in the light of his other positions and personal characteristics. Role-identities are idiosyncratic rather than cultural objects. Second, functional fit between organized sets of such idiosyncratic conceptions is considerably more problematical than that between conventionally paired social roles. For example, even though the social roles of husband and wife fit relatively smoothly, two individuals' self-conceptions as husband and as wife may greatly clash. Any pair of role-identities that fit rather smoothly are likely to be retained and become more prominent in the relationship, while any pair that does not is likely to be dropped or to fade out. In this manner the shape of the relationship is altered by the functional fit between *personas*. Third, this fit between *personas* constrains the form of interaction between the members of the relationship by, one, effectively requiring them to eschew certain actions quite consonant with their cultural role relationships but that happen to be inconsistent with a member's role-identity and, two, allowing them to perform actions that deviate from cultural role relationships but happen to be consistent with the role-identities of the members.

As previously remarked, most social relationships are a blend of formal and personal relationships. Even where role relationships are the primary guides to interaction, the members gradually acquire clues to the other's self-conceptions, from direct interaction and from third parties' reports, and come increasingly to modify the role relationship in personalized fashion. And even in personal relationships, the members may resort to culturally established role relationships in public situations or in contexts beyond the bounds of their revealed *personas*.

It should be clear from these definitions that the primary bond in formal relationships is ascription and that in personal relationships is attachment. Reward dependability, investment, and commitment operate in both types equally, although as these bonds increase in strength, bringing about further interaction, the bond of attachment typically forms and moves the relationship toward the personal type.

Consistent with these definitions of the shape of relationships are the dimensions of *social structure* typically discussed by sociologists in the analysis of larger organizations. *In the context of social relationships, these dimensions (such as affect or power) must be examined first for each pair of roles or role-identities that is included in the structure of the relationship.* Only then can the *overall* affect or power structure of the relationship be determined, *by weighting the more specific analyses according to the centrality of that role (or identity) pair* in the relationship's overall structure.

Affect structure. The affect or liking structure is often assessed in larger organizations by sociometric tests, inapplicable to dyads through the inherent limitations on the range of responses to such questions as "Which other members do you consider a friend?". The affect structure of a relationship must be approached in terms of the question "Which member (if any) likes the other more than he is liked?". This structure is less likely than the others to vary from one role (identity) pair to another and is in fact likely to be quite uniform and stable. The affect structure

basically reflects the bonds of attachment and reward dependability.[2]

Status structure. In a relationship the status structure is revealed
by determining which member (if any) respects the other more
than he is respected, over the range of role (identity) pairs.
Ordinarily the status structure is more clearcut in formal relationships than in personal. If, as most recent analyses of status suggest,
social status is determined by attributes valued by the organization, status in a relationship should reflect the bonds of investment,
commitment, reward dependability, and any superordination in
the ascribed relations.[3]

Power structure. If power is viewed as the ability to exact
compliance to one's wishes, both members of a relationship typically have some power over the other. The power structure is
then depicted in terms of power differentials: "Which member
(if any) has relatively more power than the other?". Most recent
analyses of social power attribute power to the control of resources
that another person needs or desires, in line with Waller's "principle of least interest," which holds that he who is least dependent
on other for resources maintains a power differential over other
(Waller, 1938; Emerson, 1962). Power would thus reflect differences in the bonds of investment, attachment, and commitment,
which must be evaluated in terms of alternative sources of rewards (e.g., other relationships) that are available to each member.

Authority structure. Authority, as distinguished from power,
is the *right*, rather than the ability, to exact compliance and is
typically ceded in exchange for the assumption of responsibility
for the organization's outcomes. Again, the authority struture is
more clearly developed in formal relationships than in personal.
In relationships the authority structure is discovered by ascertaining which member (if any) is accorded the right of asking the
other to comply and is determined, clearly, by ascription.

2. For a typical modern work on this and the other structures discussed
below, see Secord and Backman (1964, pp. 233–372). Liking is thought to
reflect possession of attributes valued by another person.

3. Secord and Backman (1964, pp. 23). It is interesting to note that the
presumed bases for affect and for status—possession of attributes valued by
another person and of attributes valued by the organization—are more difficult to distinguish in the case of a relationship.

Leadership structure. Leadership represents contributions to determining an organization's line of action, as by posing problems, structuring alternative courses of action, proposing solutions, and persuading members to accept or reject alternatives. The leadership of a relationship is structured in terms of which member (if any) makes greater contributions of these sorts to the functioning of the relationship. Leadership does not appear to reflect clearly differences in any of the social bonds.

Communication structure. In studying larger organizations, sociologists often examine differential rates of orginating and receiving communications. These rates vary as functions of affect and status dimensions, and leaders frequently place high on both originating and receiving. In a relationship, however, size limitations make it logically impossible for one member to place higher than the other on both rates. Given the findings in other organizations of a tendency for communications to be directed upward in the status, power, authority, and leadership structures, one might conclude that, if only one rate can be examined independently, the more useful rate is that of communications received.

Conformity structure. In most organizations conformity to the norms and decisions of the organization is not uniform among the members. In relationships which member (if any) conforms more than the other probably reflects the bonds of commitment, attachment, investment, and any subordination inherent in the ascriptive relations.

In general, most studies of social organizations have found a rather close correspondence among these seven structures. That is, a person who ranks high (or low) on one of these dimensions tends to rank high (or low) on all the others. In part, this correlation reflects causal relations among these dimensions. For example, a person high on affect, power, status, or authority is better able to provide leadership, and successful leadership consolidates his liking, power, status, or authority. The major partial exception to this correlation is the conformity dimension, where some investigators have found hints that persons high in status or low in status are somewhat less likely to conform to the organization's norms, the former because they are so secure in their position in the organization and the latter because they have very little to lose by deviating. (Homans, 1961).

One might expect that in a relationship, because of the inherent limitations on structural differentiation imposed by the small number of members, the correlation among these structural dimensions might be even greater. Particularly in personal relationships, the member who is most liked will thereby very likely be most powerful and most respected, exert the greatest authority and leadership, and initiate or receive more communication. He will have more leeway to deviate (Hollander, 1958) but is more likely to be able to structure some norms of the relationship to suit his own preferences in the first place (and therefore be less likely to deviate) (Secord and Backman, 1964, p. 334).

On the other hand, especially in broad personal relationships, position on these structural dimensions (with the possible exception of affect) is likely to vary between content areas, i.e., role (identity) pairs. The proportion and centrality of content areas in which a member is superordinate determines his position in the overall structure of the relationship. It is the fact that one member is seldom superordinate in all content areas (thus giving his partner counter power over him) that imparts the close, peerlike quality to broad personal relationships.

CULTURE

In addition to social bonds and social structure, a relationship of any significant duration exhibits a unique, emergent culture. The elaboration of this private culture is typically greater the more personal the relationship.

The goals, purpose, or business of the relationship are intimately connected with its shape and structure, being more clearcut and conventional in formal relationships and more complex and emergent in personal relationships. As in any social organization, establishing and maintaining reasonable consensus on collective goals is necessary to organizational functioning and shapes many other aspects of the culture.

One aspect clearly influenced by organizational goals is the emergent norms of conduct in the relationship. Normative expectations arise regarding appropriate activities; the division of labor (*cf.* structural dimensions); the amount, distribution, and priority of time and effort to be contributed; relations to external persons and organizations; patterns of communication and revelation; etc.

Private understandings of a less normative, more cognitive sort are also elaborated. Private terms, or neologisms, are frequently invented by the members of a relationship, bearing on its organizational concerns, and almost universally private meanings are attached to common terms. These private terms and meanings often stem from or give rise to private jokes. Yet another important type of private understanding is the unique calendar provided by the historical development of the relationship. Members frequently date events in relation to significant incidents in the history of the relationship (e.g., "it was right after our trip to Yellowstone").

SOCIAL RELATIONSHIP AS ORGANIZATION

We have seen above that relationships display several features of social organizations. First, a variety of social bonds serve to bind two persons together, providing a basis for repeated joint activity. Second, the fit between these bound elements is differentiated, structured, and thus constrains the form of the joint activity. Third, a rather complex set of understandings, a culture, unique to these bound elements frequently imposes further, more specific constraints on the joint activity.

Let us examine other features of social organizations that a relationship, as a collective unit above and beyond the members themselves, might be expected to display.

Inherent in the concept of organizational membership is the idea that personnel may be replaced without necessarily destroying the organization's structure or culture. Because a social relationship consists of the relations between persons rather than between social positions, this organizational criterion is not fulfilled in straightforward fashion by relationships; if one of the two persons is removed, the relations between them are destroyed. On the other hand, particularly in formal relationships, essentially the same *structure* of relationship may be quickly established with another alter. Even if the relationship was rather exclusive, as when a man patronized only one bootblack or one wife, he may well establish a (structurally) virtually identical relationship with another bootblack or wife. Thus, we may speak of *virtual*, but not literal, replacement of members in a relationship.[4]

A collective unit above and beyond the members can make demands upon the members, demands that may even be contrary to the members' wishes. In a relationship, the constituent *personas* or roles may in time become uncomfortable or unrewarding to their respective sponsors or occupants, but because they are the only aspects known to the other member, the persons are constrained to continue acting them out. That is to say, the structure and culture of the relationship demand that the members act in certain fashions independent of their personal desires in the matter.

A capacity for collective action, above and beyond the individual actions of the members, is yet another earmark of social organizations. Through coordinated teamwork, even a dyad, such as a pair of pickpockets or con men, may be able to achieve results unattainable by skilled individuals working separately. Furthermore, the sheer existence of a relationship may make possible some actions barred to individual persons, as when a married couple is enabled to adopt a child but prohibited from it as separate individuals.

In addition to this capacity for collective action, Goffman (1961b, pp. 9–10) has proposed five general properties of social organizations, all of which are displayed by social relationships: regulation of entering and leaving (see discussion of recruitment below); division of labor (see discussion of structural dimensions above); a socialization function (see discussion of socialization below); means of satisfying personal ends (see discussion of social bonds above); and latent and manifest social functions (see discussion of organizational dynamics below).

4. Of course, where both members are removed simultaneously, it does not make sense to speak of even virtual replacement. There must be some continuity of membership to have virtual replacement. Where continuity obtains, virtual replacement may continue through several rounds. For example, if the man who has virtually replaced his wife were to die, this wife might virtually replace him with a second husband, who might in turn virtually replace her, etc.

Although social relationships would indeed appear to be a form of social organization, they are distinguished by the peculiar feature that the members tend only poorly to perceive the relationship as a collective entity to which they merely belong. As Simmel (1950, pp. 122–25) pointed out, a member tends to see only the other person rather than a social organization.

Awareness of the relationship as a unit beyond the members is heightened when the members are dealing with or oriented toward the larger social world, which tends to treat them as a unit (McCall and Simmons, pp. 175–78). Married people are invited to events not as persons but as couples; social considerations extended to one person are often extended to his close friend as well, in recognition of their close relationship. The members themselves, recognizing their shared interests and shared fate in dealing with the larger social world, tend to act in concert rather than as individuals. Married couples, friends, colleagues typically act toward outsiders as *teams*, cooperating to maintain proper fronts. (Willard Waller (1938, pp. 383–89) has discussed these phenomena of dual participation and pair-centered interaction with insight.) In other words, awareness of the relationship depends significantly upon the salience of an ingroup-outgroup distinction.

When dealing with matters more internal to the relationship than external, this awareness diminishes and often disappears. This fact, its causes and its consequences, were brilliantly analyzed by Simmel (1950) who recognized that under most circumstances,

> each of the two feels himself confronted only by the other, not by a collectivity above him. The social structure here rests immediately on the one and on the other of the two, and the secession of either would destroy the whole. The dyad, therefore, does not attain that superpersonal life which the individual feels to be independent of himself. . . . This dependence of the dyad upon its two individual members causes the thought of its existence to be accompanied by the thought of its termination much more closely and impressively than in [a social group], where every member knows that even after his retirement or death, the group can continue to exist. . . . A dyad, however, depends on each of its two elements alone—in its

death, though not in its life: for its life, it needs *both*, but for its death, only one. This fact is bound to influence the inner attitude of the individual toward the dyad, even though not always consciously nor in the same way. It makes the dyad into a [social organization] that feels itself both endangered and irreplaceable, and thus into the real locus not only of authentic sociological tragedy, but also of sentimentalism (pp. 123–24).

The intrinsic sentimentalism brought out by Simmel is one of the most distinctive features of a social relationship (particularly of the more personal type) and can be seen in several forms.

First of all, it is seen in the *sense of uniqueness* that the participants often feel, that there has never been a relationship (a love or a friendship, for example) quite like theirs.

Closely related to this feature is the *sense of intimacy,* of giving or showing certain things only to one other person and to no one else. This emphasis is congruent with the emphasis on uniqueness, but Simmel (1950, p. 127) also pointed out how it can come, like a cancer, to destroy a relationship. That is, the parties may come to share only trivia (because these small things are not shared elsewhere and are therefore intimate) and may thus come to exclude from the relationship other parts of themselves that are more widely shared but also more important to their self-structures. The relationship itself thus becomes trivial and unsatisfying. Another danger posed by the sense of intimacy is the possibility of its disruption—which we call "jealousy" and which stems from our knowledge or our fear that some of these intimate facets are *not* being given to us and to us alone.

Yet a third aspect of the sentimentalism intrinsic to relationships is a *sense of consecration* that stems from the fact that each of the parties knows all too well that he can depend only upon the other, and upon no one else, in matters pertaining to their relationship. In a group, by way of contrast, a person's failure or odious act can be hidden behind the front of the group; he can claim to have been acting not as an individual but as an arm of the group. In a social relationship, on the other hand,

neither of the two members can hide what he has done behind the group, nor hold the group responsible for what he has failed to do.

Here the force with which the [social organization] surpasses the individual . . . cannot compensate for individual inadequacies, as they can in [groups]. There are many respects in which two united individuals accomplish more than two isolated individuals. Nevertheless, the decisive characteristic of the dyad is that each of the two must actually accomplish something, and that in case of failure only the other remains—not a super-individual force, as prevails in a group even of three (Simmel, 1950, p. 134).

And as a final aspect of this sentimentalism of the dyad, there is the unsurpassed *purity of reciprocity*. In the social relationship, in which there is no one else to hide behind or to use as a distraction, the revered norms of reciprocity in exchange, of distributive justice, (Homans, 1961, pp. 72–78) can be seen to work unimpeded by other persons. This observation does not mean, of course, that imbalances in exchange, which we ordinarily call "power" and "exploitation," do not occur in such relationships, for they do frequently occur. The purity of reciprocity entails only that such imbalances are much more difficult to conceal or legitimate than they are in more complex social organizations.

The sense of consecration and purity of reciprocity are, of course, results of the inherent limitations on structural differentiation in relationships. The senses of uniqueness and of intimacy stem from both the shape of the particular relationship and its elaborated private culture.

Organizational Dynamics of Relationships

Having made the case that social relationships are a form of social organization, I wish to examine the dynamics of relationships from the standpoint of organizational functioning. Bearing in mind the older connotation of social organization as a process of building up something (as well as the structure that results from this process), I approach organizational functioning as involving at least six interrelated social processes—recruitment, socialization, interaction, innovation, social control, and logistics. These processes are all found to operate in relationships, often in somewhat distinctive fashion.

RECRUITMENT

From the point of view of an organization, recruitment represents a process of obtaining (and avoiding) new members of the organization or occupants of social positions within it. Broadly speaking, the two major bases of recruitment are *ascription* (where all, and often only, the members of some established social category are eligible to join the organization) and *selection* (where no such *established* category defines the field of potential recruits). In societies with preferential marriage systems, for example, recruitment into a marital relationship may be determined largely by ascriptive kinship categories. In many modern societies, marital recruitment is more nearly a process of selection unguided by ascriptive categories of this sort.

These bases of recruitment exhibit some correlation (but no necessary relation) with organizational *tactics* in obtaining recruits. The most common tactic, no doubt, is to offer *inducements,* rewards of various types, including such negative rewards as coercive force or the threat of same for not joining. Common inducements to marriage include the right to sexual relations, the right to raise children, and rights to share in others' property. Negative rewards such as coercion are occasionally encountered, as in "shotgun marriages." A second common tactic of recruitment is the *draft,* in which persons are declared members without appeal to voluntaristic principles (although inducements may be necessary to exact effective performance after induction). Arranged child marriages may serve to exemplify this tactic with regard to marital relationships. In this particular context, still other tactics—such as cooptation—are more difficult to exemplify.

But avoiding certain potential candidates is equally important in recruitment as obtaining members. The most common tactic is to enforce certain *rules* (pertaining to conduct) and *standards* (pertaining to level of performance and personal qualities) for entry and continued membership. These are familiar in the marital relationship, whether ascriptively or selectively based. Demanding or frightening *rites of passage* (such as the marriage ceremony or asking permission of the bride's father) enable an organization to avoid potential candidates whose interest is not·sufficiently great. *Fees* (such as brideprice, dowry, waiting periods, and license fees) similarly deter some undesirable candidates.

From the individual's standpoint, recruitment is a process of entering (and avoiding) organizations and positions within them. Common tactics for entering include formal or informal application (such as a marriage proposal or application for marriage license), campaigning (a more active "selling" of self to influential sponsors), preparing self to meet the rules and standards of the organization, and offering inducements to the organization or some of its members.

Common tactics for avoiding entry include declining proffered inducements (often by obtaining them elsewhere or denigrating their value), preparing self to fail the rules or standards, declining a draft, and concealing knowledge of one's existence or qualities from the organization.

The impact of recruitment on an organization lies first in that the character of the organization is largely determined by the number, abilities, and interests of its members. This effect is extremely pronounced in social relationships, as the organizational analysis in the previous section makes quite clear. In fact, more than in most other types of organization, the process of recruitment actually *gives rise to* the entire organization of a relationship (particularly a personal relationship).

Additionally, secondary recruitment (i.e., recruitment not simply into an organization but into specific social positions within it) affects the degree to which particular interests become translated into organizational goals and the degree to which existing abilities and interests are effectively utilized in pursuit of organizational goals. That is to say, organizational functioning depends considerably on the fit between the division of labor and the interests and abilities of the members. Except for almost purely formal relationships, social differentiation within a relationship is almost entirely emergent and is therefore quite likely to reflect rather closely the interests and abilities of the members. On the other hand, the degree of differentiation is greatly restricted with only two members, so that secondary recruitment devices such as promotion and demotion here necessarily involve the drastic device of role reversal.

The impact of recruitment on the individual lies primarily in the effects of membership or of position occupancy on his opportunities for pursuit of personal ends. Membership or occupancy makes some goals assured, some more attainable, some more difficult, and some impossible, and it also leads the individual to define additional new goals for himself. An organization or position carries with it an entire perspective on self and the world—a set of activities, objects, standards, alters, opportunities, and motives—and it often requires the alteration, subordination, or abandonment of previous such perspectives. These effects on goal pursuit and perspectives may be profound in elaborated social relationships such as marriage, friendship, or psychiatrist-patient.

SOCIALIZATION

From the organizational standpoint, socialization is a process of training members to be functional parts of the organization, by teaching them its unique culture, especially those parts relevant to the member's position in the organization. The process involves bringing about certain changes in the member's beliefs, habits, skills, goals, values, and norms. Typically, these attributes are merely *supplemented*—added to and situationally reordered. However, for socialization into extremely demanding positions involving radical change in a person's life (e.g., the position of soldier), supplementation is inadequate and his beliefs, etc., are extensively *stripped* from him (desocialization) and *substituted for* (resocialization). Supplementation may or may not require the person to assume a formal role of learner, but stripping and substitution always do so and take place within specialized resocialization organizations (e.g., boot camp, mental hospital, prison, brainwashing camp (Brim, 1966).

The impact of socialization on the organization lies in its effects on the functioning of the division of labor and on the continuity of its culture. Even if recruitment into the organization and into its positions has been propitious, successful functioning may require that individual abilities and interests be developed, disciplined, and coordinated. Recruitment provides the raw materials for the social machine, while socialization refines, manufactures, and assembles them.

In a social relationship, particularly of the more personal type, each member socializes the other from the standpoint of his own conceptions; the process is effectively one of collaboratively *creating* the organization's unique culture, rather than simply inculcating an existing culture.

This effect follows from the fact that, from the member's standpoint, socialization represents a process of influencing the organization in order to facilitate pursuit of personal ends. Quite often this process takes the form of *cooperating* in the organization's attempts to change his own beliefs, skills, etc., since cooperation will facilitate attaining the inducements offered by the organization. In some areas, on the other hand, the member may *resist* stripping, substitution, and supplementation, by attempting to teach the organization about his own peculiarities (special abilities, experience, or defects) or about the peculiarities and opportunities of the organization of its other members.

In a marriage, for example, each member brings to it or develops conceptions of the goals, division of labor, norms, etc., that should characterize the relationship. Each recognizes that marriage will require some change in his own habits, beliefs, skills, etc., and cooperates in changing some of these. Other socialization attempts he may resist and try to counter, especially those involving stripping and substitution (e.g., having to give up casual flirting and going out with the boys, to stay home every night and wash dishes).

INTERACTION

The aspect of interaction with which we are here concerned is the various patterns, involving an organization's members (though not only members), of WHO come together for WHAT activities WHEN and WHERE (McCall and Simmons, 1966, pp. 1-2, 11-38).

From the individual's standpoint, interaction represents the pursuit of personal ends within the arena of the organization and its membership. The individual's role in the division of labor acts both as a constraint on and opportunities for such personal goal seeking. Having to wash windows may interfere with one's golf game, but marriage also facilitates attainment of sex, com-panionship, and other personal goals. Differential success in pursuit of personal goals has the effect of reshaping one's interests and self-conceptions. Interaction also serves as a discovery process whereby the individual comes to learn of members' organizationally irrelevant interests and abilities, which constitute opportunities for his own organizationally irrelevant goals.

From the organization's standpoint, patterns of interaction represent the functioning (or dysfunctioning) of the organization with respect to its own goals, norms, and so on. Of course, not all interaction involving members is relevant to organizational functioning, but that which is may either reflect or contravene the division of labor. Even that interaction itself irrelevant to the division of labor may, however, contribute to the emergence of unofficial substructures, which are powerful forces either reinforcing or subverting the larger organization.

In a dyadic relationship, of course, limitations of number make impossible any emergence of substructures. However, interaction not foreseen in the division of labor may give rise to role (identity) pairs not previously included in the relationship, thereby changing its shape.

And with respect to organizational functioning of a relationship, as Simmel pointed out, each member must actually accomplish something; there are no other members or substructures behind which he can hide his failure to accomplish his tasks.

INNOVATION

Innovation is defined here from the organization's standpoint, i.e., as social change—the introduction of relevant behaviors not envisioned in the organizational culture. For example, a wife may decide not to cook on Thursdays but to serve TV dinners. Innovations are always promulgated or sponsored by individuals or substructures, and the fate of any innovation is determined in good part by who sponsors it and what tactics he employs in seeking to have it ratified by the organization. (Ratification procedures vary widely among organizations, especially along two dimensions: democratic-authoritarian, and formal-informal.) Unratified innovations create tension in an organization, which subsides considerably if an innovation succeeds in becoming ratified, which many do not.

Somewhat independently of ratification status, innovations are viewed by other members as *creativity* (presumably reflecting unusual success in the prior socialization of the sponsor) or as *deviance* (reflecting failure of prior socialization). Deviance, of course, generates particularly high tension in an organization and decreases the probability of eventual ratification of the behavior.

From the individual standpoint, innovation represents a change in opportunity structures for personal goal seeking. To its sponsor, ratification of an innovation represents success in socializing the organization. An as yet unratified innovation leads its sponsor to engage in proselytizing, threats, withdrawal, or concealment of innovation, depending on whether other members are likely to view it as creativity or deviance. To members on whom an innovation is *imposed,* innovation effectively entails a resocialization. As noted previously, the behavior of socialization targets may range from cooperation to resistance, insubordination, or sabotage, depending on whether the innovation is ratified or unratified, deviant or creative, and on how it affects his own opportunities for personal goal seeking.

Aside from the tensions created, the effect of innovation on an organization is to bring about changes in the division of labor, goals, norms, or shared understandings of the organization.

In a relationship, innovation is both unusually frequent and unusually fraught with tension. Both these features stem from the fact that in a relationship no coalitions are available in the ratification process. Thus, the sponsor of an innovation can never be outnumbered, a situation that encourages him to innovate. On the other hand, he can have no internal backing in trying to persuade other members to accept his innovation. Without the strength of numbers, the deciding feature in the ratification process must lie in the sponsor's power, authority, or leadership alone.

SOCIAL CONTROL

Social control represents, from the standpoint of an organization, a process of reinforcement of its goals, structure, and culture. The most widely recognized tactics include *surveillance; rewards* for conformity and creativity; *punishments* for deviance and for many unratified innovations; and promises and threats relating to these three tactics. Paradoxically, rewards and punishments frequently take the form of changes in the division of labor: that is, *changing the person's position* (for better or worse, with excommunication as the extreme) or *redefining the person's role* (for better or worse).

But too many discussions of social control overplay its role as an after-the-fact corrective to deviance and unratified innovations. Social control is actually a continuous process, evident at all times, especially through surveillance, rewards, promises, tacit threats, and *rituals of solidarity.* (Incidentally, the effectiveness of even rewards and punishments is greatly widened through their ritual effect on bystanders, dramatizing the solidarity of the organization.)

From the standpoint of the individual, social control represents a constant (actual, promised, or threatened) recycling through the processes of socialization and recruitment (promotion, demotion, or excommunication). On the active side, all roles in an organization contribute to social control, at a minimum involving ritual-participation, surveillance, and whistle blowing, and often extending to the actual withholding or conferring of promises, threats, rewards, and punishments of various sorts. Nonconformists, of course, typically resort to countermeasures such as secrecy and defensive role-taking (with respect to surveillance against them) or influence attempts (to ratify their innovations).

In a relationship, social control, as the other processes, is peculiarly up to each member to accomplish. Each member must carry out not only ritual participation and surveillance but the conferring and withholding of promises, threats, rewards, and punishments. Because there is only one other member, one cannot "blow the whistle" on another, calling the attention of other members to the offender. Moreover, rewards and punishments involving the change of a person's position are highly limited, because of the minimal number of positions available in a relationship; role reversal or excommunication are the only major changes possible with respect to any role (identity) pair. Consequently, the redefinition of roles is a more frequent response. Rituals of solidarity (such as anniversary celebrations or the use of pet names) are, of course, quite common.

LOGISTICS

From the standpoint of the individual, logistics represents a process of juggling and adjudicating the various demands placed upon him by the numerous organizations to which he belongs (McCall and Simmons, 1966, pp. 187–96, 229–54). Common tactics include *scheduling* his different performances; *role segregation; audience segregation; stalling* demands; *working-in* of external role performances into the manifest role performance; *playing off* one organization against another; and *compromise* of incompatible demands (Secord and Backman, 1964, pp. 494–520).

From an organization's standpoint, logistics refers to the process of juggling and adjudicating, one, the demands placed upon it by its members and by other organizations, and, two, the demands it places upon its members (in the light of their other memberships). Its tactics are similar to those of individuals. Particularly in relation to its members, much bargaining takes place concerning the relations between the value of inducements offered by the organization and the type of demands it makes. This bargaining is strongly influenced by the respective recruitment opportunities of the organization and of its members (Goode, 1960, pp. 483–96).

In a marriage, for example, the relationship and its members are subject to the demands of external organizations such as work, kin, and friendships. The husband's friends may expect him to spend Sunday afternoon playing golf, his in-laws may expect him for dinner, his employer may expect him to finish an important report over the weekend, and his wife may expect him to put up the storm windows. Not only the husband but his marital relationship and each of the external organizations must appraise the various demands in relation to the values of inducements offered and cope with the husband's logistical tactics.

A relationship is often favored in such a situation, because of the intrinsic sentimentalism it generates in the cross-pressured individual, but it is also constrained from pressing its demands too far, because of the relative irreplaceability of its members.

The order of presentation of these six fundamental organizational processes—recruitment, socialization, interaction, innovation, social control, logistics—is heuristic only. All of them proceed simultaneously from the very beginning of any organization and obviously influence one another, as well as the bonds, structure, and culture of the organization. Some few of the directions of mutual influence among the processes have been spelled out here. In the next section, some of the organizational changes in relationships over time will be viewed as results of these organizational dynamics or processes.

Organizational Change in Relationships

Few relationships of substantial importance to their members remain unchanged for long. Such changes as may occur essentially represent alterations in the organizational components of relationships—in their social bonds, shape and structure, and culture. In each case, the changes in any component may be attributed to inherent instabilities within that component, to the organizational dynamics of the relationship, or to changes within one or both of the members.

SOCIAL BONDS

The effect of any changes in the social bonds uniting members of a relationship is to increase or decrease the strength of the binding forces—to increase or decrease the *cohesiveness* of the organization.

As I noted previously, the number and magnitude of social bonds tends to increase as a function of repeated interaction. This is most clearly the case with the bond of investment; the more often the two parties interact, the more time and resources each has invested in the other. With increasing investment, the norm of reciprocity calls for increased reward dependability from alter. A person made too dear to us through frequent rewards and our heavy investments tends to become prominent in our thinking (attachment). Commitments are sought and tendered as security on our investments. If not already present, "ascriptive" ties are sought to regularize and publicize the other bonds.

On the other hand, a genuine decrease in the magnitude of one bond tends to bring in its train a decrease in the number and magnitude of other bonds. For example, an ascriptive tie may be disrupted, as when one of two coworkers is promoted or demoted. Reward dependability of one may be thereby diminished as he is no longer in a position to provide the expected sorts of rewards to alter. Diminished reward dependability and ascriptive ties diminishes the prominence of alter in one's thoughts (attachment) and may justify withdrawal of one's commitment to alter. The rate of investment in alter will decrease, although one's cumulative investment can never be decreased; it may, however, be revalued, devaluing the worth of the investment and writing it off as a capital loss.

Other examples of this strain toward consistency among one's social bonds have been discussed earlier.

Change in any one of these bonds may stem from virtually any or all of the social processes described as organizational dynamics. Space does not permit examination of all the possible directions of influence, but several are so clearly important as to warrant mention here. The bond of ascription is clearly influenced by the continuing process of recruitment, and attachment is primarily influenced by socialization in the relationship. As I mentioned, investment is heavily influenced by interaction. Commitment is most clearly linked with social control, particularly the rituals of solidarity. Reward dependability is most influenced by the process of logistics, through which alter's limited resources are allocated among the many competing organizations of which he is a member, and by the process of social control.

Beyond organizational functioning of the relationship, personal changes within one or both members may give rise to change in any one of the social bonds (McCall and Simmons, 1966, pp. 197–201). Relevant personal changes include change in personal resources, acquisition of new standards for a relevant role relationship, change in the content of a relevant role-identity, or a shift in the hierarchical arrangement of one's role-identities. For example, alter's reward dependability may be diminished by his loss of beauty or position, and it may be increased by his acquiring a new skill. Or ego's attachment to alter may be increased or decreased by a change in his conception of self in a relevant social role. His rate of investment in alter may increase as a result of a relevant role-identity having become more important in his self-structure.

Changes in the shape of a relationship are represented by the addition, subtraction, or substitution of role (identity) pairs, by shifts in the centrality of such pairs, or by alterations in the content of such pairs.

Many sets of role (identity) pairs are not entirely mutually compatible and thus generate conflicting or inconsistent lines of action for the members of a relationship. In response to this inconsistency, the members are likely over time to alter the shape of the relationship by one or more of these three means.

Ordinary organizational dynamics also influence the shape of a relationship. Continuing recruitment, socialization, and innovation have obvious bearing upon the number, type, content, and centrality of the role (identity) pairs comprising a relationship. Logistics also has a critical effect upon the shape of a relationship. In the first instance, the sheer economy of working into the relationship as many as possible of the members' role-identities sets up a "strain toward totality" in which the relationship comes to demand increasing proportions of the members' selves and lives (McCall and Simmons, 1966, pp. 185–87; Simmel, 1950, pp. 120–22). Secondly, however, roles or role-identities that are better fulfilled in external organizations tend to become less central to the relationship and those that are better fulfilled in the relationship become more central.

Personal changes in the members, such as discussed above, exert similar influences on the type, content, and centrality of role (identity) pairs in a relationship.

Changes in the *structural dimensions,* rather than shape, of a relationship are represented by reinforcement or reversal of member's positions on these hierarchical dimensions (affect, status, power, authority, leadership, communication, conformity) within role (identity) pairs. Members' positions in the overall structure of the relationship may be reinforced or altered by such changes within numerous or highly central role (identity) pairs.

As I previously noted, there is once again a strong strain toward consistency among these structural dimensions, particularly in social relationships. Thus, a change in one dimension, such as power, is likely to induce change in other dimensions, such as leadership or communication.

Organizational dynamics or processes influence the structure of a relationship as well as its other organizational components. The continuing process of recruitment in fact *refers* to the reinforcement or reversal of structural dimensions. Social control is in good part a process of maintaining and repairing structure. Logistics exerts considerable influence on the structural differentiation of a relationship through the resulting differential allocation of the members' time, effort, and other resources to the relationship.

Personal changes in the members also affect the structure, particularly changes in a member's disposable resources. Such resources appear to be the principal determinant of position in the affect, status, and power structures, which in turn affect positions in other structures.

CULTURE

Visible changes in the culture of a relationship are perhaps more frequent than in the other organizational components. Goals, norms, private understandings, and perceptions of the relationship are continually being reinforced, undermined, elaborated, or altered. Perhaps these changes are the more visible for the fact that, unlike changes in the other organizational components, these are continually discussed and debated without shame by the members themselves, often with an eye toward directed change. When social bonds (such as investment) or structures (such as affect or power) are discussed by the members, they typically feel a sense of shame and apprehension in doing so and the very discussion constitutes some type of crisis in the relationship.

As with the other organizational components, some strain toward consistency can be noted in the area of culture, particularly with regard to the goals and norms of a relationship. Inconsistencies here generate conflicting lines of action between members, experienced as painful and costly. Changes are therefore initiated in the course of time to reconcile the various goals and norms.

Once again, ordinary organizational dynamics are quite pertinent to changes in culture. Innovation is of course the most important process and actually refers to the introduction of cultural changes. Socialization is a process of inculcating, elaborating, and shaping culture. Social control is to a considerable extent concerned with maintaining and reinforcing culture, particularly the goals and norms.

Personal changes in the members can be important influences upon the culture of a relationship. Especially important in this regard are changes in a member's conception of a relevant role (or of self in a relevant social role) and changes in a member's hierarchy of role-identities. The former has obvious implications for the goals, norms, and private understandings of a relationship. The latter is a critical determinant of the goals and perceptions of a relationship.

ORGANIZATIONAL CHANGE IN A RELATIONSHIP

The organizational components of a relationship are closely interrelated. In particular, social bonds are intimately linked with structure, as is culture. Accordingly, changes in one component are related to changes in other components.

One reason for this is that, to use the phrase once more, there is a strain toward consistency among the components of an organization. If, for example, the goals and norms of an organization are unrelated to or conflict with its structure, neither component can be effectively implemented by the members of the organization.

A second reason is that the organizational components are all influenced by the same external determinants—organizational dynamics and personal changes within the members. Thus, for example, a shift in the hierarchy of role-identities of one member may change some social bonds, the shape and structure of the relationship, and its culture.

Third, these two classes of external determinants of organizational change are themselves related. A personal change may affect the processes of recruitment, interaction, and logistics, let us say. Recruitment, socialization, and logistics also serve to induce personal changes in the member, such as in the contents of some of his role-identities and the shape of his hierarchy of identities. Personal changes and organizational dynamics thus exhibit mutual influence.

We should also note here once more that organizational dynamics stand in a peculiar relation to organizational change. Several of the processes or dynamics (recruitment, socialization, innovation, social control) are essentially names for aspects of organizational change, broadly viewed (that is, as the alteration, elaboration, and reinforcement of organizational components). At the same time it is reasonable to view organizational dynamics as having an *influence* on organizational change, since the *results* of one process of change (for example, recruitment) may effectively determine changes in some ostensibly independent organizational component (such as private terms).

Conclusions

In this paper I have attempted to establish the utility of viewing social relationships as a type of social organization, so that the theoretical frameworks and empirical results of mainstream sociology may be brought to bear in the analysis of this important but neglected class of phenomena. In doing so I have tried to identify the distinctive peculiarities of social relationships as social organizations so as to preserve the insights of imported frameworks such as role theory and interpersonal theory.

In the span of such an exploratory paper, the elements of a sociological approach to the analysis of social relationships could of course be only broadly sketched. We hope that such a sketch will suffice to guide researchers in describing and explaining the organizational components, dynamics, and change of concrete relationships or types of relationships.

We hope that other analysts will also pursue, in the context of social relationships, the question facing all students of social organizations concerning the social and social psychological mechanisms by means of which organizations effectively constrain the conduct and interaction of their members (Buck, 1966, pp. 103–72).

Boundary Rules in
Relationships and Encounters

In this essay somewhat different organizational features of social relationships are explored. The author proposes that any type of social organization may be analyzed in terms of a focus and a set of boundary rules to maintain and effectuate that focus. In this context she elaborates the idea of the *shape* (focus) of a relationship and its role in determining aspects of the culture (boundary rules) of the relationship is more clearly exhibited. Such an organizational analysis discloses an important complementarity or reciprocality between the focus and boundary rules of relationships and those of encounters, providing conceptual leverage for an understanding of the mutual effects between relationships and interactive encounters. In particular, the topics of alienation and of change in these two types of social organization are viewed from this perspective.

Largely ignored, the social relationship has occasionally been treated as an interesting adjunct to some other type of social organization—as a softening exception to theories of bureaucracy, as a kind of group, and often as indistinguishable from encounters.

35

The independence of social relationships from encounters has been particularly difficult to establish. A striking similarity of structure and process allows and even encourages treating them as inseparable. Beyond this, encounters and social relationships are related in the sense that neither exists without the other. The participants in most encounters are members of social relationships or webs of these. And one only "sees" a relationship in the encounters between its members. For example, if we observe a married couple meeting for lunch, do we call that meeting an encounter, or is it part of a relationship? And on the other hand, routinized and regular encounters are often the basis for a relationship.

The encounter and the social relationship are distinct phenomena, however, and must be treated as such, if we are to be able to analyze the important characteristics of each. A social relationship is more than the encounter between its two members. Encounters are important beyond their function as observable manifestations of social relationships.

Our interest is in the similarities of structure and process and in the interdependence of encounters and relationships, considered as two distinct types of social organization. In this paper I propose to investigate the similar structure and process of encounters and social relationships, and to go beyond previous discussions (Goffman, 1961b, 1963a) in looking at certain aspects of both. In particular, both types of social organizations have boundary rules and a focus, and they share certain processes of change.

Boundary Rules and the Focus

Among the structural characteristics of encounters that Erving Goffman (1961b, 1963a) has discussed and defined are the "focus" (1961a, p. 18) and the "boundary rules" (1961b, p. 25). He has argued that the encounter is unique among types of social organization in its possession of a focus and boundary rules. We argue, on the other hand, and this is the truly central point of this paper, that the social relationship may also be described in terms of its focus and boundary rules. We argue that the two structural characteristics appear in both encounters and social relationships and have the same overall function in each, although the form they take differs. Furthermore, certain processes having to do with changes in the boundary rules and focus are likewise shared by encounters and social relationships, again in somewhat different form. Indeed it is very likely, although that likelihood is not explored in this paper, that all forms of social organization share these structural and processual characteristics.

Two succeeding sections will treat the particular foci and boundary rules of encounters and relationships. To argue their importance to all types of social organization, however, requires a general definition of boundary rules and of the focus.

By focus, we mean the *raison d'être*, that for which the encounter or social relationship exists. Most discussions of the structure of formal work organizations include mention of what we might call the focus of these. Usually spoken of as goals (Scott, 1964, pp. 492–95), and incorrectly assumed to be unique to this type of social organization, the focus of formal work organization is, broadly, the work that gets done—the product produced or the service provided. In short, the goals of the formal work organization are its *raison d'être*. Bucher and Strauss (1961) have written of the "core activity" of professions, a related type of social organization. This "core activity" also seems to be what we mean by focus.

Boundary rules are simply norms that protect, or effectuate, the focus. The boundary rules make it possible to get done whatever must be done by excluding any potentially disruptive characteristics of the encounter, social relationship, or the larger social world and by making sure every element necessary to the focus is present. The content of the boundary rules is partially determined by existing societal norms and partially emergent. The existence of boundary rules is a part of the structure of social relationships and encounters and is thus pre-existent.

Goffman (1961b, pp. 17–34) discusses three types of boundary rules. *Inhibitory rules,* or rules of irrelevance, screen out any element in the larger social world—individual characteristics and attributes, external norms, group characteristics, and so on—that would make involvement in the focus more difficult. *Facilitating rules,* or rules of realizable resources, make sure that all such elements necessary to maintaining social order are present and used. Both facilitating and inhibitory rules, says Goffman, are really subtypes of a third type of boundary rule, *transformation rules*. He explains that elements are not merely let in or kept out. Rather, they are let in in some harmless form and are used in some most suitable form.

In addition to these three types of boundary rules of encounters, all of which deal in some way with what is "let into" encounters and social relationships, social relationships also have what I call *rules of privacy*. This type of boundary rule deals with what is "let out." That is, in order for a social relationship to exist and for its focus to be maintained, some norms must be formulated regarding the proper degree of sharing of selves with outsiders. These are rules of privacy. Encounters also have privacy rules. Most important, these rules limit sharing the focus of the encounter with outsiders, particularly in encounters that take place in public. Rules of privacy, like other boundary rules, almost certainly operate in all forms of social organization.

BOUNDARY RULES AND FOCUS OF ENCOUNTERS

Goffman (1963a) has defined encounters as "compris(ing) all those instances of two or more participants in a situation joining each other openly in maintaining a single focus of cognitive and visual attention—what is sensed as a single *mutual activity*" (p. 89). A party, a business meeting, a chat with a seatmate on an airplane, a tryst, are all examples of encounters. In each case, individuals *do* something, do participate in one "mutual activity." But nothing can be done, no human activity can proceed until the situation, the encounter, is socially organized, or defined. The definition of a situation is never wholly pre-existent, but must largely be negotiated by the participants in the encounter.

As Thomas pointed out long ago, it is the assignment of meaning in a situation that establishes the reality of any situation or encounter. Any astute observer can specify many constraints on interaction, including physical space, the statuses of actors, norms, and so on. But it is largely up to the actors themselves to specify which of these factors are to be attended to in this situation. This working definition of reality is always fragile because other factors could also be attended to, other definitions applied. All participants in an encounter must agree upon the choices and cooperate to sustain them.

The focus of an encounter, its official objects of involvement, are dictated by the definition of the situation. Individuals are spontaneously involved (Goffman, 1963a, p. 36) in an encounter when their definition of the situation agrees with the official one. But no one individual is allowed to define the situation alone. Therefore, no participant is ever wholly satisfied with the reality created. Each is forced to make compromises. A working division of labor is established whereby each individual is allowed "to establish the tentative official ruling regarding matters which are vital to him" (Goffman, 1959, p. 9). A part of the function of the boundary rules is to make sure this working division of labor comes about and is honored.

The issue of most concern to each participant is his own identity and that of others (McCall and Simmons, 1966, pp. 60–62). Each must decide "Who am I?" in this situation, and all must help to decide "Who are the others?" Because the question of one's own identity is most crucial in the encounter, and indeed must be settled before anything else can be done, the boundary rules of the encounter are most crucially concerned with identities, with letting in some, keeping out others, and transforming still others to make them utile or harmless.

The boundary rules must deal with other threats to the fragile reality of the encounter. Even such ordinary activities as bridge, a faculty meeting, or a barbecue foster and indeed require extraordinary *esprit de corps*. In order that everyone enjoy the mutual activity all must work together to build their social world. A third important function of the boundary rules of an encounter is to screen out any elements of the larger social world that would make the necessary *esprit de corps* impossible.

The participants in many encounters are not intimates. There may be wide differences among them in "wealth, social position, erudition, fame, exceptional capabilities, and merits" (Simmel, 1950, p. 46); indeed there may be great differences with regard to any social attribute. These differences must be disregarded in order that encounter-specific intimacy, or *esprit de corps,* completely necessary to the tasks at hand, can exist.

Of course, these differences may not exist, or may be harmless, if the participants in the encounter are intimates. Examples of this kind of encounter include a dinner for two lovers, or a party for old friends. In these cases, the necessary intimacy already exists. The boundary rules then need filter out fewer social characteristics that are relevant in the larger world.

Of course, certain kinds of inhibitory rules must still operate—a bad mood can spoil even the most intimate encounter—and so must some facilitating and transformation rules. But, in general, the boundary rules need not be as rigid.

As Strauss (1959, pp. 45–48) has said, intimates know what to expect of each other, within limits. Thus the boundary rules need not so carefully set limits; these already exist and are known. The problem becomes the simpler one of deciding which identities are being presented, from among a known array.

Cooperation in the creation of social reality also requires that the participants in an encounter stifle "psychological states and attitudes" contrary to the prevailing mood of encounter (Goffman, 1961b, p. 23). Simmel (1950) said simply: "It is tactless, because it militates against interaction . . . to display merely personal moods of depression, excitement, and despondency" (p. 46). Accordingly, a fourth function of the boundary rules of an encounter is the exclusion of disruptive individual feeling states.

The boundary rules perform a fifth function in rendering irrelevant any activities not part of the present encounter or not including participants in the present encounter. Preoccupation with past or future activities threatens the encounter by suggesting that the present activity is unworthy of involvement, and so this kind of preoccupation must be dealt with by the boundary rules.

The boundary rules of encounters, then, operate in at least five important ways to protect the focus of the encounter, the mutual activity. First, the boundary rules facilitate the division of labor necessary to defining the situation. Second, most importantly, the boundary rules deal with the identities of participants, and here all three kinds of boundary rules—facilitating, inhibitory, and transformation—are at work. Third, any external social differences must be inhibited, as must, fourth, contrary individual feeling states. Finally, other activities are screened out.

BOUNDARY RULES AND FOCUS OF SOCIAL RELATIONSHIPS

We have said that social relationships, as well as encounters, have boundary rules, just as both have foci. Of course, encounters involving the members of a relationship have boundary rules, just as other encounters do. But beyond this, there are the boundary rules of the relationship itself.

We have said that the boundary rules of encounters exist to protect their socially constructed realities. The boundary rules of relationships exist to protect a social construction of a somewhat different sort. Obviously, the members of relationships do not create reality in precisely the same sense that participants in encounters do. This is obvious because relationships are both more and less than gatherings of individuals. There is mutual world building nevertheless. The members of a social relationship create social organization—a division of labor, norms, power differences, communication channels, and so on—and they create a shared culture unique to that relationship (see Chap. 1). The boundary rules of a social relationship protect this reality just as the boundary rules of encounters protect the reality created there. Certainly the boundary rules of relationships are not identical to those of encounters in form, but only in function.

The form of the boundary rules of relationships differs from that of the boundary rules of encounters because relationships exist to accomplish ends different from the ends of encounters. The focus of involvement in relationships is not mutual activity but the identities of its members.

All social relationships are partly personal and partly formal. That is, the members of all social relationships interact partly on the basis of role relationships and partly on the basis of personal knowledge. Insofar as a relationship is personal, or based on recognition by each of the other, the relationship exists to provide *role support* for each (McCall and Simmons, 1966, p. 72). In its formal aspects, a social relationship may be based on reciprocal need for services, on propinquity, institutional needs and so on. But all social relationships of any duration exist at least partly to provide continuing role support for the members (p. 167 *ff.*)

McCall and Simmons introduced the concept of *role-identity,* by which they mean the way an individual thinks of himself as being or acting in a certain role (p. 67). They point out that an individual's behavior stems not from mere role incumbency but from his ideas about himself in that role. Thus two mothers might behave quite differently, depending upon how they believe mothers should act and what kind of mother each thinks she is. Beyond this, the concept implies that one's beliefs about what kind of mother or teacher or policeman one is—good or bad, run-of-the-mill or extraordinary, tough or easy, professional or dilettante and so on—require and in part derive from social support. Unless one is treated like a good mother, one cannot believe one is a good mother. And it is this social legitimation, this agreement from other individuals that one is as one thinks he is, that McCall and Simmons refer to as role support. They say: "Men seek to live and act in the manner in which they like to imagine themselves living and acting or, failing that in some degree, at least to be able to continue thinking of themselves in that same manner" (p. 151).

Furthermore, such role support must be more or less continuously forthcoming. No one ever gets enough role support; every one seeks reassurance. And new sources may refuse role support or old sources dry up. It is the necessity to serve these ever recurring needs for role support, say McCall and Simmons, that causes individuals to form social relationships (p. 167). Relationships are most simply "dependably recurring sources of role support" (p. 170).

Thus, the focus of social relationships is the identities, the role-identities, of its members and the provision of support for them. The boundary rules of social relationship are primarily concerned with activities. The focus of an encounter, on the other hand, is some mutual activity, and we have said that the primary concern of the boundary rules of encounters is with identities. Like those of encounters, the boundary rules of relationships must deal with other kinds of threats to the reality being constructed within, but their primary function is to include, exclude, or transform activities.

By definition, the purpose of a relationship is assuring continuing support for the role-identities of the members. The role-identities of the members come to require the other member for complete support. That is, "specific persons and their behaviors get built into the contents of role-identities" (p. 173). McCall and Simmons refer to this process as *attachment* (p. 172). Once a particular alter becomes part of a role-identity, part, that is, of the picture one has of himself being and acting in a certain role, this alter is "crucial to the legitimation and enactment of these identities" (p. 173).

It is a further characteristic of role-identities that they require activities—a bowler must bowl, a singer must sing—but some require only indirect activity, they may simply be talked about—a would-be author who never writes or an expert those expertise is entirely from second-hand sources are examples. It does not matter what the activity is, so long as one can gain role support by engaging in it. And because the members of a relationship become attached to one another, they must share activities in order to provide support for one another's role-identities. The boundary rules of a relationship are most crucially concerned with regulating this basic aspect of any relationship—the sharing of activities. By regulating how many and what activities are to be shared (that is, allowed into the relationship), the boundary rules facilitate the maintenance of role support, which is the focus of social relationships.

Just as the boundary rules of encounters screen out any activities going on in other encounters, so the boundary rules of relationships protect their reality, and particularly the emergent culture, by rendering irrelevant and indeed denying the existence of other relationships. Simmel (1950, pp. 125–126) pointed out that the members of relationships must believe that their relationship is unique. The members deny to themselves and to each other that they have ever known a comparable one. It is important that each believes he cannot get and cannot have gotten comparable role support elsewhere.

The promotion and protection of intimacy is a final function of the boundary rules of relationships. Probably no single relationship provides role support for every identity of any individual. The boundary rules of all relationships inhibit some identities. But the number of role-identities allowed into the relationship, and the range—whether only very conventional or very unconventional and idiosyncratic, even deviant—varies in different relationships. Following Simmel's usage, we may refer to those relationships that provide support for a wide range and very large number of role-identities as intimate relationships. Indeed, intimacy requires the sharing of role-identities in this way. Simmel defined intimacy in a relationship as the "giving and showing" of certain important parts of the self "only to the other person and to nobody else" (pp. 126–128).

Thus, those boundary rules of social relationships that we have called "rules of privacy," function importantly in promoting and protecting intimacy. For unlike facilitating, inhibitory, and transformation rules that determine what is to be "let into" the relationship, the rules of privacy determine what is to be "let out." In other words, the privacy rules mark off those identities, and attendant activities, that are to be shared only with the fellow member of the relationship, from those for which social support may be sought more widely. In this sense, then, we may say that the boundary rules of intimate relationships function to let almost all identities in and almost none out. When activities are shared and the resulting role support is sufficiently gratifying, the other who shares that activity and provides that support becomes built into the corresponding role-identity. If the members of a relationship share many activities with nonmembers and hence come to rely on these others for role support, the original relationship is in danger of becoming unnecessary.

It should be made clear that intimacy is something of an emergent quality in a relationship. We tend to think that all marriages are more intimate than all friendships, which are in turn more intimate than work relationships, and so on. While this is probably true in general, still, some marriages, for example, are more intimate than others in our sense. The content of the boundary rules of a relationship is interactively established, at least in part. Thus the quality of intimacy is somewhat emergent. The two members decide what constitutes a betrayal of the intimacy of their relationship, a break in the boundary rules, by determining those rules in the first place. At the same time, broader social norms establish what degree of intimacy is proper for that type of relationship. For example, physical intimacy is the norm for all marriages and no friendships. At the same time, some lovers decide that they need restrict only physical intimacy to themselves (and some not even that), while others refuse to share virtually any activity with a nonmember of the relationship.

We have discussed three important ways that the boundary rules of social relationships operate to protect their focus, the identities of members. First, and most basically, the boundary rules regulate the number and kind of activities to be shared by members. Second, the boundary rules screen out, in fact deny the existence of, other relationships. Third, the boundary rules regulate the number and range of identities allowed into and out of the social relationship, thus protecting and promoting intimacy.

COMPARISON OF THE BOUNDARY RULES AND FOCI OF ENCOUNTERS AND SOCIAL RELATIONSHIPS

Thus far, I have explored the structure of social relationships. Specifically, I have argued that relationships share with encounters, another type of social organization, certain structural properties—namely, a focus, the creation of a social reality to effectuate that focus, and boundary rules to protect the social reality. These aspects of the structure of encounters have been discussed previously in the literature. The contribution of this section is a delineation of analogous aspects of the structure of social relationships and some extensions of these. The remainder of the paper deals with other analogous aspects of the structure of encounters and of relationships. Before turning to these, however, we can compare in summary fashion the focus and boundary rules in encounters and social relationships.

To recapitulate, the focus of an encounter is a mutual activity; the focus of a social relationship is the identities of its members. That is, people come together in encounters in order to carry on some activity. Social relationships are formed because they offer sources of continuing support in a social world of uncertain and hard-won role support.

Boundary rules are norms, partly determined in the larger social world and partly emergent in the relationship or encounter, that make possible the activity of an encounter or the provision of role support in a relationship. The boundary rules of encounters are primarily concerned with the identities of participants. In order for the activity to proceed, everyone must know who he is and who the others are. Some identities are excluded or transformed as irrelevant or dangerous to the activity at hand. Other identities are necessary to that activity and are thus facilitated although, again, perhaps transformed.

The boundary rules of social relationships are primarily concerned with activities. Individuals become attached to the persons with whom they share activities; they come to require those persons for adequate role support. The boundary rules of relationships determine what activities will be shared, or "let into" the relationship, thus determining what identities will be supported. Equally important to relationships are rules of privacy, which determine what activities will be "let out" or shared externally. Thus the rules of privacy determine what identities will be supported externally.

The rules of privacy in relationships also foster intimacy, as do the boundary rules of encounters. The boundary rules of encounters screen out the external identities of participants, imbedded in differences in social and psychological attributes. All participants are leveled and encounter-based intimacy can obtain. The screening out of evidences of other activities also promotes intimacy; other activities are denied to protect the *esprit de corps* and spontaneous involvement necessary to intimacy in the present encounter.

The exclusion primarily of other identities and secondarily of other activities fosters intimacy in encounters and effectuates the focus of encounters, the mutual activity. Intimacy in social relationships is fostered by the rules of privacy, which restrict identities and attendant activities to the relationship. In addition, denial of the existence of other past, present, and future relationships fosters intimacy, effectuating the focus of social relationships (provision of role support) by making that role support more precious by its uniqueness.

In summary, then, encounters and social relationships are symmetrically opposite in content of focus and boundary rules. The focus of encounters is activities, and their boundary rules are primarily concerned with identities, including such evidences of other identities as contrary individual or social attributes and feeling states. The boundary rules of encounters are secondarily concerned with activities. On the other hand, the focus of social relationships is identities, the provision of role support for these. The boundary rules of social relationships are primarily concerned with activities and secondarily with other relationships and discrepant identities which, if known, might threaten support for identities within the social relationship. The boundary rules of relationships include rules of privacy; how much and what is "let out" of relationships is as important to the intimacy of relationships as what is "let in."

The following chart describes the summary differences and similarities of the boundary rules and focus of encounters and relationships.

	Relationships	*Encounters*
Focus	identities	activities
Boundary Rules		
Primary concern	activities	identities
Secondary concern		idiosyncratic moods
Make irrelevant	other relationships	other activities
Foster intimacy	by keeping out extraneous activities (and identities)	by keeping out differences in social attributes and/or letting in more role-identities to intimates

Threats to the Boundary Rules—Alienation and Change

CHANGE

The description thus far of the boundary rules of encounters and relationships and of their role in protecting a definition of reality and effectuating the focus of the encounter or relationship, has been static. It would almost seem that the process of creating a social reality, of claiming identities and deciding upon activities, happens only once during an encounter or relationship. As McCall and Simmons (1966, pp. 144–46) have pointed out, Goffman's analysis of encounters is likewise static, implying that boundary rules protect the encounter from change as well as from disruption.

McCall and Simmons, on the other hand, follow Strauss (1959, pp. 44–88) in pointing to the existence of phases during an encounter (1966, pp. 144–46). As Strauss (1959, p. 40) says, "the initial reading of the other's identity merely sets the stage for action, gives each some clues for his lines." These initial cues seldom anticipate all that will happen during the encounter. And when the unexpected happens, some adjustment must be made. The definition of the situation must be reworked, including the definitions of identity for all participants. The participants must, in Strauss' terms, take new "stances vis-à-vis one another." The encounter then enters a new phrase. "What interactional phases signify, of course, is that the relations between the actors are changing." (p. 62).

When such changes in the definition of the situation occur, the boundary rules protecting the definition of the situation must change too. Boundary rules are not fixed, but rather change during the course of any encounter or relationship. The existence of boundary rules of some sort is constant; the particular content of the boundary rules changes.

Such changes occur when one or more of the individuals engaged in the encounter or relationship becomes dissatisfied with the boundary rules. These individuals break the boundary rules, accidentally or purposefully, and the break signals a desire for change. But the individual can only *break* the boundary rules by himself; to *change* them requires a social effort. Thus, if the other participants agree that a change is necessary or even acceptable, a new phase begins. If the others fail to agree, there is a break with no remedy. In this case, we speak of a *crisis* occurring in the encounter or relationship.[1] One method of solving the crisis

1. Goffman uses the term "incidents" in his *Encounters* (1961, p. 45). I prefer this new term because of the new meanings assigned to it.

is to end the encounter or relationship; another is to exclude the offender. (In a relationship, these amount to the same thing. Since there are only two members, the exclusion of one effectively ends the relationship.) Of course, anything short of ending the encounter or relationship means that some change occurs, if only a reduction in personnel. But the enacted change may not be the one desired by the offender. The encounter or relationship has not entered a new phase. Not quite as it was before the break but unable to be anything else, the encounter or relationship simply limps along with a makeshift focus and makeshift boundary rules to protect it.[2]

Breaking the boundary rules, purposefully or not, is a rather dangerous undertaking, then. There may be a successful progression to a new phase, or there may be a crisis. Considering the danger, why do individuals break the boundary rules? The answer must be that something is important enough to them to risk failure. And that which is so important is, in encounters, simply the receipt of additional support for role-identities or support for additional role-identities, and in a relationship, the desire for additional or different activities.

In any encounter, the focus is a mutual activity and the boundary rules deal primarily with identities. Hence, changes result from demands for the introduction of new identities. Thus, the phases of an encounter do, as Strauss (1959, p. 12) says, "signify changing relations among the actors." Conversely, the focus of relationships is identities, and the boundary rules deal largely with activities. Relationships pass from phase to phase when additional activities, which result in further attachment to the partner, are included in the relationship. For example, a purely work relationship between fellow employees becomes a personal relationship when they begin to share leisure-time activities. Or a

---

2. There seems to be some sort of internal time-table for these things. At a certain point, the question of becoming lovers comes up in most cross-sex relationships. At a certain point the ladies stop playing cards and turn their full attention to gossip. If a young man and woman do not become engaged after a certain period of courting, it becomes clear that they never will—although they may not see this. When a relationship, in particular, does not progress in this way, it becomes abnormal in some sense and probably less satisfactory to its members.

personal relationship may pass through the phases labeled friendship, lovers, marriage. The direction of change may be toward the inclusion of fewer identities or activities, of course. But particularly in healthy relationships, new phases are usually brought about by inclusion of more activities.

Phases in Encounters. New phases in encounters result when the boundary rules governing the claiming and accepting of new identities are broken. Individuals break the boundary rules when they are dissatisfied with the encounter and sometimes simply because it is necessary to do so.

There are two kinds of dissatisfaction with the boundary rules of encounters, particularly those boundary rules that deal with role-identities. On the one hand, all individuals are always dissatisfied in a general way. There are compromises involved in the definition of the situation. No individual is ever allowed to claim as many role-identities as he would like. Every actor is always on the lookout for opportunities to get support for as many role-identities as possible. New phases of encounters often come about because some actor seizes upon such an opportunity. Probably such opportunities arise most often as a response to some claim made by another actor. In the process of deciding whether *his* claim is valid, one may oneself have a chance to make additional claims. A suburban housewife who wishes to justify her opinions during a discussion of art, for example, may allude to her college major in art.

But beyond this sort of universal and general dissatisfaction, there may be very specific dissatisfaction with the role-identities one is allowed in the encounter. For example, an individual may feel that he cannot perform the required activity sufficiently well to maintain the self he is forced to present. Or he may feel that he has been cheated, as it were, in the allocation of allowable role-identities. The individual will in these cases seek to change his self, to gain support for different or additional role-identities.

Often it is necessary for the actor to claim additional statuses. Ego may make a claim that is not relevant merely on the basis of role-identities thus far claimed, alter may challenge his right to do so, and ego is thus forced to present appropriate other role-identities. For example, an individual might claim expertise and then have to show his credentials. On the other hand, the mutual activity may necessitate some additional claims—someone to score at bowling, someone to sing or tell a joke at a party. Very often in this case, an actor urges another to claim this status. (And that actor who does the urging is responsible for the break in the boundary rules as much as is the actor urged. Actors seem to feel this responsibility, being just as eager as the performer to see that the activity is performed well.)

Phases in Relationships. A rather large literature deals with the whole question of phases in relationships. Farber (1964) has dealt with the careers of marriages and families, Davis (1961) with phases in the relationship between normals and the handicapped, Roth (1963) with work careers and the phases of work relationships. McCall and Simmons (1966, pp. 167–201) have discussed the general question of the phases of social relationships. We will not here consider the phases of relationships in great detail, but a few general remarks are in order.

There seems to be a movement toward totality in relationships, analogous to the chronic general dissatisfaction with role-identities in encounters. This is a general dissatisfaction with activities in relationships. Individuals who have a relationship almost inevitably begin to share more and more activities. This is caused in part by the requirements for intimacy in relationships, discussed above.

Specific dissatisfaction with the number or type of activities allowed in a relationship also leads to change. One member who wishes to share an additional activity may signal the other; if they agree, a new phase begins. For example, one coworker may suggest that the other have dinner with him; if the second agrees, they are sharing leisure time as well as work activities, and their relationship has moved away from the formal and toward the personal.

The attempt to add activities is not always successful, of course. One member may not want the relationship to enter a new phase. Furthermore, there are institutional constraints on the progression to new phases in some kinds of relationships. For example, the ethics of doctors, lawyers, and other professionals require them to limit relationships with clients to the formal and to leave aside the personal (Parsons, 1959). Where successful, however, the inclusion of additional activities in a relationship causes the relationship to enter a new phase.

ALIENATION

We have, in the treatment of phases, discussed the general question of a desire for change in the boundary rules of an encounter or social relationship, some of the dangers in proposing such changes, and the results of successful and unsuccessful proposals. In this section we will discuss the related question of alienation from the focus of an encounter or relationship.

Goffman (1967) defines alienation from encounters exclusively in terms of involvement with the focus of the encounter. An alienated individual is either involved in some other focus or not involved spontaneously in the official one. Goffman uses the term "misinvolvement" synonymously with alienation (p. 117).

We follow this usage to the extent that we refer to *dissatisfaction* with boundary rules, but *alienation* from a focus. Thus, a participant in an encounter may be dissatisfied with the number and kinds of identities allowed him and if he seeks change, he initiates a new phase in the encounter. But if he is alienated, it is because he dislikes the activity he is engaged in and if he seeks change it is a change in the activity. Likewise, a member of a social relationship may be dissatisfied with the number and kinds of activities shared with his partner, but alienation from the relationship involves the identities for which he gives or receives role support.

We depart from this usage, on the other hand, in refusing to make rigid distinctions between dissatisfaction and alienation in terms of their manifestations and results. Both are manifested in breaks in the boundary rules, being but two kinds of impetus to change in the encounter or social relationship. Furthermore, the two are not always easily distinguished empirically.

If an individual is not a good bridge player and daydreams during a game (and he could not be a good player if he did daydream), it is not at all clear whether he is alienated from the focus of the encounter or whether he is also dissatisfied with the self he is being called upon to present (bridge player) and is breaking the boundary rules in order to cause change in these rules.

Similarly, because additional shared activities necessitate additional support for identities, it is difficult to separate dissatisfaction with the boundary rules from misinvolvement with the focus in relationships. An individual who is alienated from the focus of a relationship, unhappy with the support he is receiving or being called upon to give, often seeks new or additional role support outside the relationship, thus breaking the boundary rules of privacy.

We make the distinction between alienation from the focus and dissatisfaction with the boundary rules because it does seem at least intuitively meaningful to expect that in social relationships, dissatisfaction with boundary rules will lead to increasing intimacy if efforts to change succeed, whereas alienation from its focus will bring about a lessening of intimacy. As we have previously said, healthy relationships tend toward increasing intimacy. Likewise, alienation nearly always leads to some lessening of intimacy, even though the alienation is hidden or changes do occur (McCall and Simmons, 1966, pp. 197–201). One might imagine a relationship that becomes less intimate the more satisfied its members, or one in which alienation leads to increasing intimacy. If such relationships exist, we are not concerned with them here. We suspect that it is unhappiness with one's own or the other's identities and role support which brings about alienation in the sense of a withering of the social relationship, whereas dissatisfaction with boundary rules most often stems from a desire for "more" of a relationship.

Alienation from Encounters. Alienation from an encounter includes spontaneous involvement in another focus (even in the focus of another encounter) as well as lack of spontaneous involvement in the official focus of the present encounter (Goffman, 1967).

An alienated or misinvolved participant may follow one of three courses of action. First, he may hide his alienation and continue to participate while alienated. If the alienation remains hidden, it constitutes a psychological problem, which we are not interested in here. It is true, however, that such a feeling state tends not to remain secret. It will almost surely be reflected in the performance of the individual. Even if it is not discovered, he will almost always make his displeasure known eventually.

Thus, *discovery* and the *revelation* of alienation are the other two possible courses of action open.

An alienated individual may be discovered. Goffman (1963) provides an example in his discussion of an "away" participant who is caught with his attention wandering. He suggests that this is particularly dangerous because it causes other participants to suspect that the guilty party has been guilty during the whole encounter and that he cannot be trusted not to err again. We shall refer to this as *causing a scene*. The result of causing a scene is either to bring about change in the encounter or to precipitate a crisis in the encounter. That is, the offender may be forgiven but his self remain suspect, as in Goffman's example. In this case, there is change in the self assigned to him, if not in the self claimed. Or the guilty individual may have to claim a new self, thus breaking the boundary rules again.

The third possibility for an alienated participant is *making a scene*. That is, an individual may purposefully make known his alienation from the focus of involvement. For example, one player might say, "I don't like playing pool, let's play billiards instead." The two possible consequences of *making* a scene are identical to the consequences of *causing* a scene. The individual may be unsuccessful in his efforts to change the focus of the encounter, in which case there is a crisis which must be dealt with in some other way or the encounter is ruined. If the individual is successful, the focus is changed, but he may also bring about changes in the self that others assign to him and perhaps in the kinds of activities they invite him to participate in. A change in the focus of the encounter may necessitate changes in the boundary rules.

The relationship between alienation and desire for change in an encounter should be clear. Unless an individual is to remain covertly alienated, there must be a scene, which in turn may either lead to change or to ruining the encounter. Likewise, as we have said, a dissatisfied participant, one who wishes to change the boundary rules of the encounter, will break the rules in order to *signal* this desire for change. Thus in either case there will be some threat to the social reality created by the encounter's participants. And in either case there will be either change or a spoiled encounter as a consequence.

Alienation from Relationships. Just as change in relationships is analogous to change in encounters, so is alienation from relationships analogous to alienation from encounters. We have discussed the desire to change the boundary rules in relationships; since the boundary rules of a relationship deal primarily with activities, change involves the addition or exclusion of activities. As we have said, the focus of a relationship, its purpose, is the maintenance of role support. Individuals form relationships in order to have reliable sources of support for their role identities. Thus alienation from relationships entails some lack of involvement in shared role-identities. The two principal types of alienation are defined by two important types of involvement. In order for the relationship to "work," each member must want role support and each must be able and willing to provide it. An alienated member may not want role support or he may be unable to give role support. (The reverse cases—the individual whose support is refused or the one who cannot get support—will be considered in passing.)

1. Does Not Want Role Support. An important subset of the boundary rules of a relationship dictates what activities are to be let out, as we have seen. These boundary rules protect the identities of the members by guarding against the possibility that outsiders will get built into role-identities simply because they are included in activities. The member who finds that he can get role support outside a relationship often becomes alienated from that relationship. If he is getting support for the same role-identities both inside and outside the relationship, but finds that the support he receives outside is more satisfactory, he may well decide he does not want or need the support his relationship partner gives. In this case he feels alienated; he is not involved in the maintenance of support provided in the relationship. A related possibility is perhaps even more common. One member of the relationship may be getting support outside the relationship. If these role-identities become more important to him, then the support he receives outside becomes more important and he may become alienated from the relationship.

One very common type of alienation occurs most often in formal relationships. A role-identity may become less important to an

individual, rendering the relationship that provides support unimportant too. One might be an avid fisherman or golfer or
thespian for a time and share an important relationship with
fellow fishermen, golfers, or thespians. Very often the interest
passes and the relationship with it, often without a scene of any
kind. This type of alienation is most common in a relationship
based on a single role-identity. If the relationship is based on
many role-identities, as personal relationships are, the loss of
involvement in one may not be crucial. It might happen, however,
that one member loses interest in only one of many role-identities
but that role-identity is basic to the existence of the relationship.
Alienation of this sort results.

Loss of interest in receiving role support will also result if an
individual becomes alienated from a particular role-identity or
set of role-identities. If, for example, the relationship is built upon
role support for esoteric or even deviant role-identities, and these
role-identities are rejected, the relationship will almost certainly
be rejected, too.

Separation is a common cause for the loss of desire for support.
Far from making the heart grow fonder, or the relationship
stronger, separation often necessitates the pursuit of support
outside the relationship. And, again, this outside support may
become more important than the support within the relationship,
particularly if the separation makes it the only support directly
received. An interesting subtype of this kind of alienation may
result from what might be termed "setting segregation." Some
relationships are setting-specific. That is, they flourish in some
specific locale, but are often not transferable to another locale.
Shipboard romances, college friendships, and neighbor relationships often end when the members separate.

When one member of a relationship becomes alienated in the
sense that he no longer wants support for role-identities, the
other member whose support is refused often tries harder to provide support. Each member of a relationship probably receives
some gratification from giving support, but each also realizes he
will not get support without giving it. The member who perceives
the other's refusal and senses the threat to support for his own
role-identities may try to arrest the deterioration. This is usually

a delaying tactic at best, because the already alienated member resents the increased offering of support. One hears it said, "He won't give me up" or "She won't let go."

2. Cannot Give Support. The second type of alienation from a relationship is the inability to provide support for the other's role-identities. One partner is reluctant to allow into the relationship some role-identity for which the other desires support. The reluctance may stem from disapproval of a highly idiosyncratic or deviant role-identity and a consequent desire to minimize its importance to the other.

On the other hand, the reluctance to allow some role-identity into the relationship may be simply the result of an effort to avoid a more "total" relationship. Alter may feel that ego wants to be "too close a friend" or too "dependent" a spouse. He will then wish to avoid giving support for any additional role-identities, however innocuous.

The individual who cannot get role support may react by increased pressure for support. This is a sort of misinvolvement, too—an over-involvement with the seeking of support. The frustrated partner may turn to another relationship for the support that is not forthcoming in the current one.

As with encounters, alienation from relationships may be hidden, revealed, or discovered. This is true of both types of alienation from relationships which we have discussed. An individual may *hide* his feelings, he may *cause* a scene, or he may *make* a scene when he cannot give or does not want role support.

Attempts to hide alienation from a relationship are generally as unsuccessful as are attempts to hide alienation from encounters. The alienated individual almost always reveals his feelings in the end, although often not until he has established a new relationship to replace the unsatisfactory old one. The discovery of alienation, rather than its purposeful revelation, is as devastating to a relationship as it is to encounters. Not only are present and future interactions threatened, but past interactions are spoiled as well.

In spite of the almost certain destruction of social relationships when alienation is either revealed or discovered, individuals alienated from relationships may be more likely than alienated participants in encounters to choose to reveal alienation than to try to hide it. It appears that alienation can be endured long enough to "get through" an encounter. A relationship, by its very nature a long-term phenomenon, cannot be so easily endured in this sense. Of course, as we have said, there are degrees of alienation. Perhaps, then, an individual must be more alienated from an encounter before he reveals his alienation and need not be as alienated from a relationship in order to make his feelings known. In any case, this is probably not true in all societies at all times[3] but rather depends upon the ease of forming new relationships as well as societal beliefs about the endurability of unsatisfactory relationships.

Of course, such cross-cultural and historical comparison does not negate the basic point here, that an individual alienated from an encounter or a relationship may either hide or reveal his alienation, and if he hides it, he may be discovered or not. On the other hand, analysis of the relation between alienation from encounters and from relationships *does* reveal that the existence of the one type constrains the choice of how to handle the other. For example, it is impossible to reveal or discover alienation from an encounter with a relationship partner without thereby threatening the relationship too.

Interrelations Between Alienation from Encounters and from Social Relationships. As we have said, encounters and relationships are closely related types of social organization. A social relationship between participants affects any encounter between them. And the encounters in which members of the relationship participate affect that relationship. In this same sense, the social relationship will be affected if either member is alienated from an encounter between them. And alienation from the relationship will make encounters between members difficult. This reciprocal effect is obvious if one remembers that the boundary rules of relationships deal with the very matters that are the focus of encounters and vice versa. Misinvolvement in the focus of one constitutes a break in the boundary rules of the other. Such a

3. Farber suggests that in contemporary American society relationships are ended rather easily as soon as they become unsatisfactory (1964, Chap. 4 and pp. 167–69).

break signals the desire for change in the boundary rules, and the attempted change may be successful or may result in a crisis. In short, alienation from an encounter may cause a crisis in a social relationship and vice versa.

For example, if the members of a relationship are alienated, they may be unable to sustain an encounter without making or causing a scene. Seeing one's ex-lover for the first time is such a case. (The two persons may be helped if there are other participants in the encounter.) Second, the existence of a relationship may disrupt an encounter if the members are so involved with each other that it constitutes a lack of involvement in the official focus. Finally, alienation from an encounter may affect relationships. If the members have an unpleasant, unsatisfying encounter, they may become alienated from the relationship itself, particularly if the encounter has as its focus some activity central to the relationship.

This reciprocal effect means that there are constraints on the choices of how to handle alienation, as we have said. An individual who values the relationship he shares with another participant in an encounter may decide to hide his alienation from the encounter rather than risk spoiling their relationship by revealing it. Likewise, one member of a relationship may hide his lack of spontaneous involvement in the support of some role-identity rather than risk spoiling a valuable encounter by breaking its boundary rules. For example, a husband may treat his wife as a knowledgeable political partisan at a party, even though as a general rule he is not spontaneously involved in providing support for that role-identity in their relationship.

It is wrong, of course, to assume that individuals always choose to hide alienation from encounters to save relationships and vice versa. Individuals may reveal alienation from an encounter to force a change or even to cause a crisis in a relationship. (The reverse case may be true but is unlikely). And in any case, the choice is not simply between hiding and revealing alienation; it may be simply discovered. The discovery of alienation from an encounter is at least as potentially dangerous to a relationship as is revealed alienation. An individual who is not spontaneously involved in the focus of an encounter or relationship is breaking the boundary rules of the other's organization, and the discovery of that break necessitates some adjustment of the boundary rules at the risk of a crisis.

Conclusions

This paper has analyzed some aspects of the structure and processes of social relationships. We have used concepts developed by Goffman for the analysis of encounters. Indeed, we have maintained that the two types of social organization are closely related in structure and process, despite differences in form and function. Disagreeing with Goffman, we have argued that social relationships as well as encounters have both a focus and boundary rules. We have proposed a fourth type of boundary rule—rules of privacy that deal with what is "let out". The three types of boundary rules discussed by Goffman, displayed by both relationships and encounters, deal with what is "let in."

The focus of encounters is activities and the boundary rules that protect the focus deal primarily with the identities of participants. Conversely, identities and the provision of role support for them is the focus of social relationships. The boundary rules of relationships deal primarily with activities that are essential to such role support.

We have suggested that other types of social organization, particularly formal work organizations and professions, also have foci. Indeed, these have been discussed in the literature under various names. We hope that others will explore the possibility of boundary rules in types of social organization other than encounters and social relationships. Certainly the existence of such a similarity in structure would not be surprising, if indeed all the phenomena we consider social organizations are indeed of a type.

Further analysis and research is also needed as to the differential genesis and effects of dissatisfaction with boundary rules and alienation from foci. Our analysis here constitutes a bare outline. The question of whether individuals become dissatisfied with the boundary rules of other types of social organization must be answered elsewhere as well.

A further question, particularly interesting to this author, is whether the forms of collective behavior, an interestingly deviant type of social organization, share the components of structure and process discussed here. Particularly, is there a relationship between the partially societal and partially emergent nature of collective behavior and of boundary rules?

Certainly this discussion of boundary rules and focus constitutes only a partial analysis of social relationships. Other papers in this book deal in detail with other components of the social relationship as a type of social organization.

Rules of Conduct and the Study of Deviant Behavior: Some Notes on the Social Relationship

The culture of social relationships is the central subject of this third essay as well, but with an emphasis on the moral order. The ordinary codes of propriety are shown to be distinctively transformed within what the author calls "relationships of substance," serving to circumscribe deviant behavior and to insulate the individual from societal reactions to his deviance. At the organizational level, the author describes how this distinctive moral order bears on alienation and change for both relationships and encounters. He recounts devices of social control characteristic of social relationships.

At the heart of any social order lies a bundle of recurrently validated rules of conduct (Goffman, 1967, pp 47–95). Ultimately derivable from some set of values or preferred lines of action,

Abridged and revised from a somewhat longer version in Jack D. Douglas (ed.), *Deviance and Respectability: The Social Construction of Moral Meanings,* New York: Basic Books (1970). I am indebted to Evelyn K. Denzin for suggestions and reactions to earlier portions of this essay.

these rules specify for the participants appropriate and inappropriate ways of behaving toward that group's valued social objects. A rules of conduct is, then, a guide for action that is recommended not because it is "pleasant, cheap or effective, but because it is suitable and just" (Goffman, 1967, p. 48). The existence of such rules impinge on daily conduct in two fundamental ways. First, they specify *moral obligations* of conduct. They define the moral character of social selves and when employed establish their users as upholders of the social order. When a husband cooperates in celebrating the anniversary of his marriage by purchasing a gift, he at once celebrates the basis of his relationship while reaffirming his commitment to that relationship.

Second, rules specify the types of *expectations* ego may hold alter to. Patterns of deference, or avoidance and presentational rituals, reference the obligatory feature of rules. Nurses, for example, may expect to receive orders from physicians, but cannot in turn give such orders (Goffman, 1967, p. 49). The rules of conduct governing their relationship are thus *asymmetrical* and if a nurse violates this asymmetry she challenges the sacred value of the relationship and the attendant selves involved.

Thus, when rules of conduct are violated both parties run the risk of embarrassment and self-discreditability. Both actor and recipient are threatened, for their selves have not been upheld. A central feature of rules of conduct—can be noted—they are daily reaffirmed through the rituals of interaction and communication. They adhere not so much to participants as to the situations and occasions of interaction. Their meaning arises only when persons translate them into ongoing lines of action. To be precise, rules of conduct are *situationally and relationally specific.*

These rules may take many forms. In the past, two generic types have been treated. The first are those formalized into laws and enforced by specialized bodies, such as the police and the courts. I call these *rules of substance,* or more properly, *rules of the civil-legal order.* These formalizations, which may be expressed by law, official morality, or codes of ethics, commonly govern conduct in public settings and exist to protect the objects designated by them.

It is these rules of the public–civic order that have most centrally concerned Becker (1963) in his analysis of the outsider. In turn, his examination of these rules has given rise to the recent concern of the sociologist with social control agencies and the public deviant.

Goffman (1963a) on the other hand, has focused on what may be termed ceremonial rules, or rules of *civil propriety*. These are specifications that guide conduct in matters felt to have secondary importance in their own right. Their official function is to maintain the moral and social order of those expressing them. These are commonly viewed as rules of etiquette. They govern polite, face to face interaction among persons when they are in both public and private behavior settings and may range from statements on proper dress to how one introduces himself to a stranger. In these rules and their violation Goffman derives his theory of mental illness. He suggests that what is meant by mental illness is behavior that routinely and regularly violates the rules of polite, situational face-to-face interactions. Hence he speaks of the structure and function of situational proprieties and delineates such rules as those governing the acquaintanceship process, body idiom, visual interaction, face work and so on.

It is suggested that there is a third category of rules that Goffman and Becker have not attended to, and these are what may be called *rules of relationships,* or *relational proprieties*. In enduring, long-term social relationship those categories of rules Goffman has categorized under civil proprieties become radically altered, redefined, and at times irrelevant. For example, Goffman discusses the way males and females in our society attempt to control the information they give regarding themselves in another's presence. He states:

> Before entering a social situation, they often run through a quick visual inspection of the relevant parts of their personal front, and once in the situation they may take the extra precaution of employing a protective cover, by either crossing the legs or covering the crotch with a newspaper or book, especially if self-control is to be relaxed through comfortable sitting. A parallel to this concern is found in the care that women take to see that their legs are not apart, exposing their upper thighs and underclothing (1963a 26–7).

Rules of this order are classified by Goffman under requirements of *body idiom* and involvement shielding. He implies from his treatment of this rule that it represents a rule of behavior that governs all persons whenever they are in another's presence. He uses data from his observations in mental hospitals to demonstrate their violation:

> The universality in our society of this kind of limb discipline can be deeply appreciated on a chronic female ward, where, for whatever reason, women indulge in zestful scratching of their private parts, and in sitting with legs quite spread, causing the student to become conscious of the vast amount of limb discipline that is ordinarily taken for granted (1963a, p. 27).

I suggest that these rules are daily violated in enduring social relationships. Not only among persons labeled mentally ill—it is not at all uncommon, for example, for married males in our middle class society routinely to expose the upper portions of their body on a sunny weekend afternoon when working on their lawn. Nor is it uncommon for married males and females drastically to relax the rule of body scratching when enjoying an evening of television. In fact, it is not at all unusual to see either the female or male in various stages of undress when they are preparing for an evening at the concert, or in the last preparatory stages of a dinner party at their own home. In short, enduring social relationships not only sanction the violation of situational rules of civil propriety, but in fact these relationships are built on a deliberate violation of such rules. This of course is not meant to suggest that marriage represents flagrant violations of all rules of conduct—this is not so—and in fact as representative of one class of relationships, marriages are built on a unique order of moral and civil rules—that which is not allowable in polite society is now sanctioned.

There exists in our civil society a category of behavioral rules that have as yet not been systematically examined. They are rules of relationships and represent rules that in some indirect yet systematic fashion represent analogs to the previous two categories of rules. Further, the violation of relational rules frequently leads a given set of audience members to impute deviance to an ongoing set of interactions. Rules of conduct have relevance and meaning only when they are fixed in specific interactional and relational contexts. The categorical statement that groups have rules of conduct, without an interactional–relational specification on the part of the investigator, makes the notion of deviance by labeling at the very least a vacuous statement.

I turn now to the nature of social relationships. Briefly, I shall indicate that relationships are of a wide variety, the rules attached to them are widely varying, and the rules that grow up around them in fact represent specific translations of civil–legal and polite interactional standards into the morality of the relationship. In addition, I suggest the conditions under which relational partners will come to view the other as deviant and hence enact rules defining him as some "sort" of deviant.

The Nature of Social Relationships

That a good deal of daily human interaction takes place in either the *symbolic* or *physical co-presence* of another cannot be denied. Despite the recurrent regularity of this phenomenon, sociologists still lack the appropriate imagery and symbols to conceptualize the wide degree of variation that occurs when humans carry on recurrent interactions. Simmel (1950, pp. 118–135) defined the dyadic relationship as one in which strains toward totality, intimacy, and sentimentality are present. Weber (1947, pp. 118–20) paralleled this position when he defined a relationship as existing when there was a high probability that two or more persons would come together in co-present interaction. Cooley's (1956, pp 23–31) distinction between the primary and secondary relationship represented one of the few attempts to introduce a qualitative distinction into this concept. The vast theoretical and research literature on the other—reference group and otherwise—has contributed to our understanding of those relationships that are abstractly symbolized but not actualized in daily, face to face interactions.

Even Goffman, the one contemporary sociologist who has persisted in analyzing forms of co-present interaction, has been too limiting for our purposes. His world of study fundamentally constitutes interaction among the unacquainted, the stranger, and only infrequently the friend. His human beings are actors, ever on a stage searching for "action" and dramaturgical support. Seldom does he offer a picture of social man caught up in "safe-patterns of interaction," in which his front could drop and he might for the moment feel at ease. Given this bias, it is not surprising that his attention would fall upon rules of etiquette and their functions for polite interaction. In a world where no one can trust the other, protective devices must be created to save the moral worth of these tenuous objects called selves.

Becker, on the other hand, has extensively examined the rules of conduct that adhere to ongoing relationships, but his focus has been on the deviant. Hence, there is in neither of these theorists a throughgoing concern with daily forms of recurrent interaction among persons who are not outsiders or in some other sense a public deviant.

My thesis is as follows: the range and types of social relationships that characterize human interaction have remained largely unconceptualized by the sociologist. Sociologists have yet to describe adequately the effects of such relationships and to sufficiently come to grips with how these ranges of experience are created, stabilized, and dismissed by persons themselves.

I take as my problem, then, the study of the social relationship and its effect on the creation of private and public forms of deviance. My perspective is that of the "acting other" and I shall assess the effects of these experiences as the persons involved perceive them.

SOME DISTINCTIONS AND DEFINITIONS

A relationship exists between two or more people when those people engage in recurrent forms of either symbolic or co-present interaction. The emphasis on symbolic deserves special attention. For a relationship to exist the parties involved must share the same or similar set of reciprocal definitions about the other. Further, these definitions must extend through time so that the influence of the other does not disappear when he is out of physical, face to face presence.

There may be those relationships that exist on merely a symbolized level—with face to face interaction never occurring, or having once occurred, does no longer. The widowed wife's continuing love for her deceased husband is one example; the minister who daily speaks with a higher being, the student who carries on internal conversations and dialogues with his absent professor, are others. I call these *relationships with the absent other.*

There are those relationships that combine face to face recurrent interactions (e.g., co-presence of other) with symbolized images of the other. The love relationship described by Simmel is one example. The marriage dyad, the employer-employee relationship, and the friendship between close acquaintances are other instances of this type of relationship.

I have distinguished two basic types of relationships; those that exist on the purely symbolic level and those that combine the symbolic with recurrent face to face interactions. Additional definitions and distinctions are in order. Earlier I defined a relationship as a condition represented by reciprocality of interaction and/or symbolizations of the other. It is apparent, however, that this statement must be modified. There are those relationships that are not reciprocated on either a symbolic or face to face basis. The wife who carries on a dialogue with a deceased husband is in no way engaging in a reciprocated relationship. Her dialogue is only in the form of an internal forum or discussion with that other. He never speaks out directly. Teenagers who belong to fan clubs represent another instance. Letters to their idol are returned by a secretary and not the idol himself. And even though the idol may strongly influence such personal matters as dress and vocabulary, the influence on the fan is indirect. The employee who idealizes his relationship with an employer is another type of the *unevenly reciprocated relationships.*

Clearly any relationship between two parties will never represent *unilinear* reciprocation. The idealized romantic love theme in American culture, which describes two lovers forever intertwined in an enduring relationship, represents an ideal few relationships ever attain. It is possible to speak, then, of relationships that are reciprocated and those that are nonreciprocated. Further, there are those that are reciprocated, but unevenly so. Thurber's description of the Walter Mitty complex represents this type.

When a person is in a reciprocated relationship, no matter how unevenly, he is said to be *in relationship.* The marriage dyad illustrates this case. Husband and wives are not expected to be looking for other relationships of the sort represented by marriage. They are locked in that relationship, notwithstanding what may be the differential commitment and involvement of each in it. Frequently persons "in relationships" will find themselves for a period of time *out of that relationship.* The wife who leaves for a vacation while the husband remains at home places her husband in the uncomfortable position of both being in and out of the relationship at the same time. The symbolic demands of the relationship remain constant, but the important element of physical co-presence has been removed. Middle-class morality abounds in tales of the indiscreet husband who acted "out of relationship" when his wife was gone.

In some instances persons find themselves "in between relationships"—the "searching" divorcee, the broken engagement, and the man out of work. In such instances, peculiar symbolic demands are present. Having acquired the perspective and vocabulary of the previously "involved other," the person feels a sense of internal collective behavior; not knowing whether to drop that perspective completely or to search again for a similar other. Friends and acquaintances of such persons also feel peculiar demands. Fearing the potential embarrassment that may arise by bringing up the absent other, they do not know how to handle this peculiar person.

A peculiar type of "constrained freedom" falls upon people in this category. They are permitted to search, be indiscreet (up to a point) and even on occasion are permitted to bring up that other in conversation. These are the moments of revealing truth when the harsh reality of relationships come to the surface. To have embedded one's self in another's personality and then be forced to withdraw that self is painful. All people, at one time or another, fear such occurrences and are painfully sensitive to the demands of those who suffer through such occurrences.

Additional types of relationships can be noted. There are those that are idealized, as in some marriages and love affairs, those that are nonreciprocated and rejected, those that are over and past, and those that are purely symbolic yet recurrent in a symbolic sense. In addition, there are those that are reciprocated, yet truncated in either a situational or role-specific sense. The employer-employee relationship, for example, is both situated by time and place. Consequently, in these instances, we find both parties locked into only a few identities or images of self. The relationship has a restricted effect on the selves of both parties. Further, there are longstanding relationships, reciprocated on both the symbolic and co-present levels, and those that are longstanding and non-reciprocated or unevenly reciprocated. The bartender-customer relationship may be longstanding, but only unevenly reciprocated.

TIME, PLACE, AND INVOLVEMENT

To recapitulate, I have suggested that relationships may be ana-lyzed by their duration, location, and degree of mutual involve-ment. Those relationships that are time-specific, place-specific, and involvement-specific represent what we commonly observe in encounters with strangers, employers, civil and legal authorities, clients, customers, colleagues, and passing acquaintances. On the other extreme, a relationship existing beyond specific situations, of long duration and resting on many levels of involvement, repre-sents the case of friends, lovers, and relatives. Yet such a distinc-tion, while conceptually attractive, is much too gross. It is beyond the scope of the present discussion to treat each of these relation-ships in the detail they deserve. My purpose has been to suggest the tremendous variety of relationships that may be generated and briefly to distinguish analytical dimensions for treating them. It is now necessary to return to the theme of deviance and the re-lationship. But first, I must examine the morality of relationships.

Unless otherwise indicated, the types of relationships I shall discuss are those in which multiple identities are evoked and are of long duration, typically enacted in a variety of situations. Para-digmatically I am treating what Cooley called primary relation-ships and what I call *relationships of substance*—marriages, long friendships between colleagues, mutual acquaintanceship, and the like. In this essay I ignore any detailed treatment of the stranger relationship, the fleeting encounter between the unacquainted, as well as the highly formalized relationship in the bureaucracy (Wood, 1934). I deal with the relationships one enters with confi-dence, feelings of safety, sincerity, and at times intimacy.

Analytically my discussion will be heuristic and more suggestive than definitive. In the areas of interaction and deviance under analysis little in the way of systematic evidence may be brought forth. I hope to develop a framework that will permit others more comprehensively to treat an area that heretofore has received little attention.

Relational Morality and Propriety

Each social relationship may be viewed as a peculiar moral order, or a social world, to use Shibutani's term (1962, pp. 129–147). Contained within it are special views of self, unique vocabularies of meaning and motive, and most important, symbol systems that have consensual meaning only to the participants involved. In relationships of long duration rules surrounding the following dimensions will be developed. First, rules specifying acts of deference and demeanor that direct the participants' behavior when he is both alone and in public. Second, mechanisms for regulating knowledge, secrecy, and personal problems endemic to the relationship. Third, task structures to specify who does what, when, where, and with whom. Last, specifications concerning the proper conduct of ego and alter when not in the other's presence.

These are interactional dimensions on which rules of conduct will be built. Their existence serves to give order, rationality, and predictability to the relationship. I suggest that violations of these specific rules leads relational members to feel embarrassment, irritation, annoyance, and at the severest extreme self-threat and publicly designated deviance.

Before turning to these dimensions of the relationship several other characteristics must be noted. First, each relationship represents a universe of social experience and discourse unique to those involved. The meaning of a nonverbal gesture, of the trite phrase "I love you," of time, past occurrences, and broken selves are all contained within these little worlds.

Second, relationships may validate, redefine, or make irrelevant rules from any other moral order, be they civil–legal, polite propriety, or another relationship of the same class. Herein lies their signal importance for the student of deviance, for they represent the ways members of any society make that society's rules of conduct meaningful in their daily interactions. Hence, each social relationship potentially contains a set of deviant values and ideologies, which, if ever made public, would brand the member-participants as outsiders and deviants.

Third, the rules of conduct on which these relationships rest fundamentally refer to how the social self is to be defined and treated. To sanction the violation of a rule of etiquette is to say that for the selves involved such rules are irrelevant.

Fourth, these relational rules of conduct and their attendant moral orders are neither *situationally* nor *personally abstract*. They have reference only within the context of the relationship and are shaped and altered every time a new participant, new situation, or new problem arises. Thus, partners in marriage may not sanction quarreling in public, viewing it as indiscreet and character-damaging for their relationship. Yet they will surely quarrel in private and are quite likely to sanction quarreling between other people although they may well apply their own relational rules to that couple and brand them as *relationally deviant* for the transgression. They are unlikely, however, to make this interpretation public to the perceived transgressors.

This brings me to the fifth point. By applying their relational rules to others, members of a relationship establish their own uniqueness and reaffirm the rationale for the rules' existence. Thus, married partners can point with fond pleasure to the embarrassment felt by a quarreling couple in their presence and pride themselves for their sense of character propriety.

Sixth, by applying relational rules to others, people uniquely uphold their society's general values. That is, while they may reject a specific rule of etiquette or civil–legal rule, they have replaced that rule with another that permits them to act orderly and quite frequently within the boundaries of permissible public and private behavior. In a very general sense, no societal value or rule of conduct is expected to be perfectly enacted and followed. American society in fact allocates rewards to those persons who have reinterpreted its values in unique ways. Thus, for example, while an outlaw motorcycle gang systematically violates nearly every imaginable rule of propriety, some part of society at large rewards them for their specialness and their sense of character, charm and style (Thompson, 1966). They are simultaneously branded as deviants and heroes. But in this peculiar definition observers see brought forth the unique translatability of rules of conduct. One can be highly rewarded for publicly disavowing them if he does so with character and style.

The severe societal reactions that fall upon the rapist of course represent the other extreme. While he may do what many males secretly desire, his action lacks the style and character to bring upon him both distaste and honor. Problems seem to arise for the mentally ill, the indigent, the mentally retarded, and the occupationally and educationally incompetent.[1] We can find little in the way of glamor in their actions; and if we did, few of our moralities would sanction such actions.

Seventh, since relationships develop their own moralities and special world views, they quite soon begin to take on a life of their own. In short, an element of supra-individuality emerges and settles down and around the member-participants (Simmel, 1950; McCall and Simmons, 1966, pp. 167–201). Marriages, for example, immediately have forced upon them not only the values of their members but special values from the broader society. It is assumed that marital partners do certain things and assiduously avoid others. This element of supra-individuality leads to a number of important consequences. First, for all persons involved, a special sense of self is evoked and created. Second, an implicit demand is placed upon each person to maintain that moral order—often times at great personal loss. Goffman phrases these demands as follows:

> It seems to be a characteristic obligation of many social relationships that each of the members guarantees to support a given face for the other members in given situations. To prevent disruption of these relationships, it is therefore necessary for each member to avoid destroying the other's face. At the same time, it is often the person's social relationship with others that leads him to participate in certain encounters with them, where incidentally he will be dependent upon them for supporting his face. Furthermore, in many relationships, the members come to share a face, so that in the presence of third parties an improper act on the part of one member becomes a source of acute embarrassment to the other members. A

1. That societies create "surplus populations" for purposes of upholding occupational, moral, and ideological structures is suggested in Farber (1968, pp. 3–42, 260–71).

social relationship, then, can be seen as a way in which the person is more than ordinarily forced to trust his self-image and face to the tact and good conduct of others (1967, p. 42).

An element of trust and reciprocality thus develops in the relationship. I shall indicate shortly that refusals to validate this moral order may leads to feelings of rejection, embarrassment, lack of trust, or only general irritation on the part of one or both of the relational partners.

A third consequence of this supra-individuality in the relationship is that rules will develop to permit relational release, or escape from its demands. These rules of release may be of any duration, and as in divorce be forever binding. At cocktail parties marital partners may momentarily release the other from certain restrictions and thus permit conversations and actions not otherwise sanctioned. These are episodes in which nonself conduct is sanctioned. However, a very restrictive sense permeates these episodes, for no matter how free the release is, the person is ultimately held accountable to his actions during this sequence: his actions must always relate back to his major relationship. Hence, his actions, while reflecting momentarily on a nonself, ultimately reflect on his relationship and the character of the other self that permitted his conduct. People all stand to lose a great deal when their relational partners act to excess in nonself episodes.

Fourth, just as all relationships build in conditions for release, so too do they develop procedures for handling and preventing embarrassment. Thus, when a husband engages in an extreme nonself episode, the wife typically has at her disposal a variety of motives and explanations to account for that conduct. On occasion, however, nonself episodes will be so severe to prohibit any reasonable explanation being attached to them. In these situations the relationship may virtually collapse and abruptly disappear from existence. Even if such severe consequences do not occur, many relational partners hold this threat over their partners.

Thus, we see that a sense of security and fear at once permeate all relationships. If people step too far out of bounds it may disappear. If they are judicious and careful, the sense of security that adheres to these social orders will be maintained, often past their own lifetimes.

Given these characteristics of the relationship, I can now turn to the rules surrounding deference, demeanor, knowledge, tasks, and public behavior.

DEFERENCE AND DEMEANOR IN THE RELATIONSHIP

Each social relationship, whether at work, at play, or among friends, contains specifications (often implicit) of deference and demeanor for the involved participants. Deferentially, rules restricting avoidance and presentational conduct and in acts of demeanor standards of modesty, sincerity, and discretion appear as ways of permitting the appropriate selves to be presented.

These rules may be *symmetrical* or *asymmetrical,* as when wives defer to their husbands' role (Goffman, 1967, pp. 47–95). Their enactment reveals the underlying morality and vocabulary of the relationship as can be seen in the case of a wife deferring to her husband. Both deference and demeanor may be expressed, not out of respect, but because of custom or tradition, or for dramaturgical reasons. Thus, an employee may call his employer by a nickname out of his presence but when they are face to face employ a formal term.

The two categories of deference that deserve special attention are the *avoidance* and *presentational rituals.* By avoidance rituals I refer to norms governing "how far one can intrude into another's personal space." Each of person is located in a sacred space, with himself at the center; elaborate rules operate in American culture to permit some persons into that space ard to keep others out. Thus marital partners, new lovers, and old friends can differentially caress, pat, and otherwise touch the other's body. Each relationship has its own avoidance rituals, which may go no further than specifying that secretaries and employers sit at nonintimate distances from one another.

Presentational rituals of deference involves the use of special salutations, "touch systems," and different ways of noticing the other's presence and thereby according him the status deemed necessary and appropriate. The use of nicknames among friends implies a degree of sincerity, intimacy, and prior acquaintance. To use a nickname or first name when a formal name would be appropriate denies proper respect to the recipient (Gross and Stone, 1963, pp. 1–15).

Through acts of deference ego conveys to alter his sense of respect. He communicates to him what kind of self he has defined him as being. Through acts of demeanor ego establishes the definitions of self he wants alter to validate and give deference to. By dress, style of speech, nonverbal gestures, and on occasions through direct declarations people stake out their interactional identity.

Taken out of a relational context, deference and demeanor have little relevance for my analysis. But by viewing each relationship as an unique moral order it can be seen that within each exist special rules of deference and demeanor. Special "touch systems," manners of dress and undress, the use of nicknames, salutory rituals, and other presentational strategies grow up within them. When in relationship and alone the members will be expected to adhere strictly to these rules. *When in public these rules will undergo translation and as such will dictate the collective presentation of selves of the members.* Thus, rules of deference and demeanor ascribed to relationships by outsiders will constitute for those outsiders their basis of classifying that relationship.[2] Conversely, they will specify for the outsider how he is to act toward the members—individually and collectively. In short, relationships take on a supra-individual quality and membership in them provides a source of labels and directives for action by both the insider and the outsider.

PROBLEMS OF KNOWLEDGE

Not only does each relationship evolve rules of deference and demeanor that direct their own and others' behavior, but specific strategies for controlling knowledge about the relationship are established (Simmel, 1950, 307–76; Goffman, 1959, pp. 77–237). By controlling the amount and type of knowledge it gives off publicly, a special sense of *respectability* is sought and maintained. To achieve this respectability or *dramatic idealization*, the relationship finds that it must classify the range of situations and

2. In this sense we are suggesting that membership in a focal relationship represents for any person a "master status" that overrides virtually all his other involvements. See Becker (1963, pp. 32–33) for a discussion of master statuses and the attribution of deviance.

persons it comes in contact with as either safe or unsafe, trustworthy or untrustworthy (Goffman, 1967, pp. 141–44). These rules are often implicit and never formally voiced. Yet across situations and audiences specific attempts will be observed to monitor the kinds of information given so that a *specific definition of the relationship is maintained.* Not only are audiences and situations classified, but so too is knowledge about the relationship. Some topics are simply taboo to outsiders and hence subject to the strongest rituals of secrecy. These may range from *dark secrets* out of the past; *strategic secrets* integral to the relationship's ongoing existence and performances; and *inside secrets* made known to a select few. (Goffman, 1959, pp. 142–43)

When discrepant information leaks out, potential problems are imminent, and under these situations we can predict that attributions of deviance will arise, both from the inside and the outside.

TASK DECISIONS

A sense of *dramaturgical collusiveness* is likely to develop around the relationship also to dictate how its work is to be handled, both privately and publicly. Husbands and wives may have private and public divisions of labor so nearly opposite that role reversals can be observed at certain times. Because each relationship creates its own divisions of labor outsiders viewing that relationship perceive varying senses of familiarity and unfamiliarity, comfortableness and uncomfortableness, depending on the particular arrangement.

NONRELATIONAL CONDUCT

Rules, again implicit, develop to govern a participant's behavior when he is not in the presence of alter. Typically aided by an elaborate symbolic order, relational partners find that they can convey their relational status nonverbally. (Thus marriage rings or a well-kept demeanor can convey for the female varying degrees of the marital status.) For the male, being clean shaven and well dressed represent two strategies of communicating marital status and occupational security.

Communicating one's relational status poses several problems. First, if correctly located, one finds that he must act "as if" his relational partner(s) were present. In these situations, conversational strategies and interactional maneuvers become severely restricted or widened, depending on the perspective. If the incorrect relational status is imputed similar problems may arise. A person may deliberately masquerade as another type of person and wish to be labeled as "out of relationship." This seems to be the case for the following categories: married males searching for homosexual contacts, married males "looking around", males looking for another job, married females looking for another partner.

When sociologists examine nonrelational conduct, they must simultaneously keep in mind the perspective of the relationship being presented (or not presented) and those viewing the presentation. There seem to be ritual occasions when one can look for another relationship without recriminations (conduct at conventions, in certain bars, on vacation, and so on) but once involved in a relationship, a person finds that he is basically held accountable for that relationship wherever he goes. Relational partners thus develop strategies for communicating their status when they are out of the other's presence and hold alter accountable to the same rules.

Problems for the relationship arise when the partners fail to agree on these rules, and under these circumstances varying degrees of relational impropriety will be perceived, again by both the insider and the outsider looking in.

Perceptions of Relational Impropriety

I turn now to the issue of *relational impropriety*. The basic question guiding the discussion will be "Under what conditions do relational partners define themselves and others as deviant?" I am led to this question by virtue of the earlier propositions, which held that relationships redefine society's legal and moral orders and that many forms of public and private deviance find their locus in the relationship.

THE RELATIONAL CONCEPTION OF DEVIANCE

To answer the pivotal question, a number of related issues must be treated. First, I must make clear my conception of deviance. I agree with the labeling theorists and define deviance as any behavior so defined by the self or some set of others. I restrict this definition, for the moment, however, to *relational deviance. That is, misconduct that is not formally treated or recognized by the broader society or its social control agencies.* Conceiving deviance in this relational fashion leads to a continuum of potential deviant reactions appropriate to any relationally perceived act.[3] The range of reactions to any set of actions may take any or all of the following forms. At the most extreme end of the continuum are publicly acclaimed, validated, and legislated labels of deviant. The criminal, the sexual deviant, and the political anarchist represent this form of the societal reaction. Next are those deviant acts that are regarded as *self-threatening* or *character damaging,* but the reactions to them are handled interactionally and seldom made public. Criticisms of dress, drinking behavior, or nearly any self-attribute fall in this category. Third are those errors that cause *embarrassment* to those present and involved in the action at hand (Gross and Stone, pp. 1–15). Loss of poise, the presentation of an inappropriate identity, or the misinterpretation of alter in an interactional sequence give rise to embarrassment, and again these are problems that are handled interactionally, often through rituals of avoidance. Fourth are those actions that are *irritating* but not embarrassing. For females these often take the form of criticizing another's sense of style and fashion. For males it may include irritation at another's drinking patterns, style of speech, and so on. Clearly it is not possible to restrict these to sexual dimensions. The point to be made, however, it that various locations in the age–sex–status structure of one's society leads one to view actions by certain others as inappropriate, incorrect, and irritating. Interactants typically handle irritation by ignoring it or staging situations in which the likelihood of such occurrences is significantly reduced.

Fifth are those actions that all people engage in, feel bad about afterward, and hence attribute no sense of disapprobation to the actor. Drinking to excess, repeating a favorite story, falling into a mood, and the like represent these occurrences. They are the

3. Cavan (1961) has suggested a continuum similar to our own; however, her bias is in the direction of formal–societal reactions.

daily taken-for-granted actions that we all engage in and dutifully accept on the part of others.[4]

Sixth are those actions perceived as legitimate, ordinary, and routine within one interactional sphere but when viewed from the outside may evoke public labels of deviance. What criminologists term "white collar crime," and what members in an organization perceive as ordinary, represents this category of relational deviance. Dalton has elaborately described actions such as this. He reports the following instances of what would be viewed as misconduct by certain outsiders (Dalton, 1959, pp. 199–205).

> A foreman built a machine shop in his home, equipping it with expensive machinery taken from the shop in which he worked. The loot included a drill press, shaper, lathe and cutters, drills, bench equipment, and a grinding machine.

> The foreman of the carpenter shop in a large factory, a European-born craftsman, spent most of his workday building household objects—baby beds, storm windows, tables, and similar custom-made items—for higher executives. In return, he received gifts of wine and dressed fowl.

> An office worker did all her letter writing on the job, using company materials and stamps.

> An X-ray technician in a hospital stole hams and canned food from the hospital and felt he was entitled to do so because of his low salary.

> A retired industrial executive had an eleven unit aviary built in factory shops and installed in his home by factory personnel. Plant carpenters repaired and reconditioned the bird houses each spring.

Commenting on these actions, Becker illustrates the above points concerning relational deviance:

> Dalton says that to call these actions theft is to miss the point. In fact, he insists, management, even while officially condemning intramural theft conspires in it; it is not a system of theft at all, but a system of rewards. People who appropriate services and materials belonging to the organization are really being rewarded unofficially

4. In one sense this form of deviance is represented in Garfinkel's (1967, pp. 35–75) investigations of routine deviance in daily interactions.

for extraordinary contributions they make to the operation of the organization for which no legitimate system of rewards exist . . . The X-ray technician was allowed to steal food from the hospital because the hospital administration knew it was not paying him a salary suffi-cient to command his loyalty and hard work. The rules are not enforced because two competing power groups—management and workers—find mutual advantage in ignoring infractions (1963, p. 126).

Bringing actions such as these to the public eye involves the kind of complex negotiations that *moral entrepreneurs* are so skilled at. I shall only incidentally be concerned with those fullblown reac-tions, however. *My interest thus lies in the more ephemeral interactional reactions of embarrassment, self-threat, and irritation that routinely occur when social relationships are brought forth in emergent encounters and occasions.*

SYMBOLS, ENCOUNTERS AND OCCASIONS:
WHENCE THE ACTION?

The statements above on the nature and evocation of relational misconduct suggest that the reality of a relationship exists only on the occasions when their members present themselves for public interaction. In some senses this is correct; that is, the co-presence of two or more relationships in a behavioral situation necessarily gives rise to an interactional encounter. In these encounters be-tween relationships we observe the confrontation of varying moralities and proprieties and herein lies a part of what Goffman (1967, pp. 149–270). calls "the action."[5] That is, in these encoun-ters, which typically evolve into occasions or *gatherings of signifi-cance*, the approbations of deviance and misconduct arise.

But relationships have other realities as well. Of equal signifi-cance are the symbols people carry around that represent their characterizations of the selves, moralities, and relationships that they and others are involved in. Man, I am suggesting, maintains a sense of security and predictability in his interactions by fondly

5. Contrary to Goffman's view, which sees "action" occurring in the race car, on the stage, and on top of a mountain, we suggest it lies instead in the vibrant moral orders and interactional encounters between relationships.

isolating certain images of self and other in his mind and recurrently calling forth these images. To use Cooley's phrase, "the other exists for us in our imaginations of him." In these internal and silent conversations, we stake out views of self, challenge the other's morality, test lines of action against his perspective, and carefully prepare ourselves for the next set of interactions with him.

Placed within the context of relationships, it is possible to see that each participant carries around images of that relationship in his mind and routinely governs his conduct by these symbolizations. Conversely, he transposes those images on all other persons he encounters who are defined as being in the same "kinds" of relationship as he. These perspectives are derived from focal relationships.[6]

Given these conditions, it can now be seen that in any given encounter, whether within the same relationship or when relational partners confront others, the symbolic images of what is "right and proper" govern any conceptions of misconduct that emerge out of that encounter.

MISCONDUCT WITHIN THE RELATIONSHIP

Earlier it was noted that rules of conduct develop around the dimensions of deference, demeanor, knowledge, tasks, and "in-public conduct." I suggested that because relationships take on a life of their own, each member feels obliged to sustain that moral order—to some degree on all occasions, public or private. In addition, I noted that perceptions of relational deviance may range from feelings of "this is routine" to irritation, embarrassment, extreme self-relational threats, and public accusations of deviance. Taking the role of any relational member, the following conditions can be hypothesized as giving rise to perceptions of misconduct.

The first and most general hypothesis states that misconduct is perceived whenever any relational member fails to uphold the

6. See Shibutani (1962) on this point. We have avoided employing his conception of social world because it implies interactions with any "other" who may share some interest in a person's activities. Thus he applies the concept of world to interest groups, cults, political parties, occupational groups, and so on. While we adopt many of Shibutani's notions of the social world as a referent for interaction, we have restricted its abstractness and termed it a moral order.

moral order of his relationship. Generally speaking the *routine, taken-for-granted* and hence "forgivable" reactions occur when a relational partner acts on a rule that is unclear, forgotten, or infrequently evoked. This seems to be the case when errors of public etiquette are violated; when a husband calls his wife by a long-forgotten nickname; and when a relatively unimportant date is forgotten (e.g., a distant relative's birthday). Under these conditions, initial feelings of minor or faked irritation may appear but soon disappear when the transgressor explains his mistake. These are the kinds of interactional errors that daily surround interactants and keep them mindful that everybody forgets or is occasionally impolite.

Feelings of *irritation* arise when the relational partner fails to aid the other member in carrying off a routine act, or when a member acts to excess in an area that has little consequence for subsequent interactions. Thus, the husband who expects his wife to initiate laughter after his favorite joke and finds that his spouse has become engrossed in another conversation will feel mildly irritated but not likely embarrassed.

Embarrassment, which is the most interesting case, seems to arise when a relational member enacts an inappropriate identity, loses poise during a public encounter, and/or makes the wrong interpretation of the situation and those present. (See Gross and Stone, 1963, pp. 1–15)

Enaction of an *inappropriate relational identity* may arise when a husband violates a deference or demeanor rule. Thus he may become excessively attentive toward his wife when having drinks with friends and cause embarrassment to both relationships. To his relationship, embarrassment arises because he has publicly violated their "personal touching code" and in a very direct sense has involved his wife in a silent sexual act now public. To those looking on, several degrees of uneasiness are likely to be felt. Should they counterreact by similar "touching" actions? Would it be appropriate to suggest a termination of the encounter? Can they discreetly avoid "noticing" the action going on before their eyes? Can they shift the encounter to a mutually engrossing topic and hence "lift" the transgressors out of their impropriety? These represent at once interactional strategies and repressed reactions the viewers are likely to feel.

Such encounters generate a peculiar interactional tenseness for no one is likely to verbally give notice to the misconduct. An encounter is thus likely to ensue which is entirely nonverbal. Given the peculiar meanings often attached to the same nonverbal gestures it is quite probable that no one will know for sure what the other is thinking.

In one sense, the evocation of an inappropriate relational identity increases the probability that one or all of the persons involved will suffer a loss of poise. Speaking of poise and the individual actor, Gross and Stone (1963, p. 6) state: "Personal poise refers to the performer's control over self and situation, and whatever disturbs that control, depriving the transaction, as we have said before, of any relevant future, is incapacitating and consequently embarrassing." Loss of poise, I suggest, deprives the enacted relationship of the deference and appreciation it desires and demands from those viewing its performance. This is so because if any one of the relational selves is challenged, the collective self of the relationship is also challenged. Hence relational partners stand to lose a great deal when one of their attendant members begins to act inappropriately in public.[7] Private transgressions are of course a different matter. In these situations embarrassment is likely to be felt if an absent other is symbolized and brought forth in the encounter. To bring that other into the transaction is to make it public in some degree, even if he is not physically present. Hence, it is not uncommon to hear the phrase "Don't you ever do that in public!"

Several conditions can give rise to a loss of poise, and hence to embarrassment. The *situation* can be misread, hence leading to situationally inappropriate conduct. Thus students in the home of their professors may act overly personal and drop their usual formal-name basis with the faculty. On these occasions, reciprocal embarrassment is felt (if the act is viewed as incorrect) and both parties draw back into themselves and deliberately reduce the "openness" of the occasion. On other occasions relational partners may find that they are without the usual *props* they employ when staging performances for visiting teams. Hence, on a particularly

7. In this sense we view relationships as performing teams. See Goffman (1959).

important occasion they may find themselves without liquor, appropriate "snacking" materials, or the kind of music that would make the encounter flow as desired. On other occasions the wrong props may be present and thereby foster a definition of the relationship that is out of character. On these occasions, both relational partners will feel uncomfortable and perhaps even embarrassed. The presence of liquor and drinking equipment before friends who do not drink raises an inappropriate identity structure for both parties. Commenting on the role of props for such occasions Gross and Stone note:

> The porcelain dinnerware may always be kept visibly in reserve for special guests, and this very fact may be embarrassing to some dinner guests who are reminded that they are not so special after all, while, for other guests, anything but the everyday props would be embarrassing. Relict props also present a potential embarrassment, persisting as they do when one's new life situation has been made obsolete. The table at which a woman used to sit while dining with a former husband is obviously still quite serviceable, but it is probably best to buy another (1963, p. 9).

Loss of poise may also arise when the relational partners have inappropriate *equipment* present during their encounters. Following Gross and Stone I distinguish props from equipment by the degree of mobility accorded them during an occasion.

> If props are ordinarily stationary during encounters, equipment is typically moved about, handled, or touched. Equipment can range from words to physical objects, and a loss of control over such equipment is a frequent source of embarrassment. Here are included slips of the tongue, sudden dumbness when speech is called for, stalling cars in traffic, dropping bowling balls, spilling food, and tool failures (1963, p. 9).

On certain occasions faulty, noisy, inappropriate, and otherwise intruding forms of equipment challenge the character and selves being presented. On the evening of a prenuptial dinner the author observed an unusual intrusion of equipment from the outside that challenged the ritual nature of the occasion. A former boyfriend of the bride-to-be's sister had been circling the house for several hours, peering into the back yard where the dinner was being held. The yard had been strung with Japanese lanterns to give the effect of a graden party and suddenly, just as toasts were being offered to the couple-to-be, the boyfriend crashed into the light-pole and brought all of the lanterns down with sparks and explosions. Collective behavior spread, curses filled the air, rapidly followed by profuse apologies from the mother of the bride to all the guests. While lights and order were soon restored, the ritual nature of the occasion had been so severely challenged and damaged that it soon collapsed. The mother felt she had been offended by a "punk teenager," but most importantly her presentation had been damaged and the sacred character of her family and soon-to-be married daughter had been severely flawed.

A fourth factor that may lead to relational embarrassment is the presence of incorrect dress on the part of one or both of the members.

> *Clothing* must be maintained, controlled, and coherently arranged. Its very appearance must communicate this. Torn clothing, frayed cuffs, stained neckties, and unpolished shoes are felt as embarrassing in situations where they are expected to be untorn, neat, clean and polished (Gross and Stone, 1963, p. 10).

On any given occasion each relational partner is expected to be in dress such that a consensual definition of the relationship can be conveyed and maintained. Being out of dress thus challenges the definition and gives rise to potential embarrassment to all persons involved. In some situations the failure to pay due respect to another's dress can create mild feelings of embarrassment and irritation. A new dress that goes unnoticed by a close friend may lead the presenter to be irritated and regard the viewer as inconsiderate. The failure to notice new, novel, and uniquely arranged equipment and props can also create this reaction. A sensitive feel for the importance of these objects and a knowledge that one accords deference by ritually noticing their presence leads some relational partners to develop a division of labor in this regard. Thus, wives are expected to notice new furniture, drapery, tableware, and the like, and husbands may be given the territory of books, records, and mechanical devices. It is possible to observe peculiar forms of cajoling and "notice-taking rituals" in this respect, for one partner may notice an object in the other's domain and subtly call it to the other's attention. In some settings the owner of the object calls attention to its presence and here the rituals of deference are tightly drawn. Having an object called to one's attention requires that one can properly respond. Thus, conversational strategies of a quite traditional variety are brought forth and such phrases as "Oh, how nice!" or "I wish we had that!" can be observed.

A last condition that potentially gives rise to relational embarrassment is the failure to keep one's body under proper control. This of course relates to the earlier discussion of the relational touch system and rules of deference.

> The body must always be in a state of readiness to act, and its appearance must make this clear. Hence any evidence of unreadiness or clumsiness is embarrassing. Examples include loss of whole body control (stumbling, trembling, or fainting) loss of visceral control (flatulence, involuntary urination, or drooling) and the communication of other "signs of the animal" (Gross and Stone, 1963, p. 10).

In any relational social structure, normative standards arise to specify correct and incorrect body control. The intentional or unintentional violation of these rules thus challenges the ritual order of the presented relationship. Few effective strategies are available to cover these indiscretions. While such motives as fatigue, drunkenness, and boredom can be evoked, they seldom work. Typically what is observed is the designation of such conduct as "nonself" behavior. Placing it within this category also implies that it is "nonrelationally" relevant, and all persons can be absolved of responsibility when exposed to the episode. On some occasions an entire phase of an encounter will be written out of existence. All members agree to forget what went on. It was a nonencounter. Expressions of grief, extreme drunkenness, and overaffection seem to fall in this category. These are strategies, however, that may or may not work. The fact that they are called into existence suggests that the character of the presented relationship has been severely challenged.

Feelings of *self-threat* are more severe than reactions of irritation and embarrassment. In those situations when the ritual and moral value of the self is challenged, the entire relationship underpinning the self is severely damaged. It seems axiomatic that all the conditions that create embarrassment also can create self-relational threats. Thus, unnoticed props and equipment, misidentified selves, improper body control, and dress lead back to the relationship itself.

But more important, there is in these actions a disconcern for the relationship itself. This raises the question of conduct when out of the physical presence of alter and when one is in-between relationships.

Husbands who behave indiscreetly, wives who flirt with other males, employees who derogate their employers, and children who tell "tales" behind their parents' back convey by their actions a basic disrespect for the relationship they are representing. These are situations where relational-release cannot be sanctioned and hence the actor must be held accountable for his misconduct. On these occasions the character of one's own relationship is threatened, for if husbands respond in a like manner to an indiscreet wife, they open the way for similar actions by their own spouse. In short, they are forced to condone these actions if they do not respond in a recriminating manner.

When a person commits an act defined as inappropriate to the moral order of his major relationship he is most likely to be defined as a relational deviant. Indiscreet husbands, fiances who cheat, employees who steal, and children who "rat" on their parents soon find themselves defined as untrustworthy. Extreme avoidance rituals are enacted, exclusion to friendship circles begins, and they soon learn that they have transgressed a very important ritual order. Having once traveled beyond that outer boundary of respectability they may never return. Search as they may for the old friends and the trusting wife, they will soon find that for them that relationship is over and done. In short, they have dangerously broached the territory of the public deviant. On occasion they may be permitted to return, but, as Jackson (1962, pp. 472–92) has shown with the alcoholic, having once left, things are never the same upon return.

Perhaps more than any other kind of transgression, the relational threat makes all persons aware of the fragile order of their moral worlds. One has only to read the daily lists of divorces and letters to Dear Abby to be reminded of this fact.

Several conditions potentially give rise to a perceived relational threat (Spitzer and Denzin, 1968, p. 463; Denzin, 1969, pp. 930–31). First, the behavior of one of the relational members may change over time and lead to a breakdown in the accommodation patterns between that person and the other members of the relationship. A father who enjoys poker parties with his cronies may increase his involvement in this activity so that he spends only a few nights a week at home. Soon his children and spouse begin to feel excluded from his interactional circle and counter by excluding him from their affairs. Almost without notice, it may occur to both parties that all sense of accommodation has collapsed and a relationship of substance no longer exists. Both respond by charging the other with inappropriate conduct and unless counter forces are established the relationship may collapse. Similar problems seem to occur with the wife who displays signs of mental illness, the drinking father, and the married man who insists on working eighty hours a week at his office.

Second, the potential deviant may bring his actions to the eyes of influential outsiders and their perceptions are then fed back into the relationship. Social workers, physicians, close friends, distant relatives, and even legal authorities may take on such a role (Sampson *et al,* 1962, pp. 88–96). The veracity of their definitions may thus lead the other relational members to view the potential deviant's actions in a different light. They may attempt to foster changes on his part, and if he is unsuccessful in validating his actions, ascriptions of deviance may appear *within* the relationship. Under these circumstances, the moral order of the relationship is challenged and unless changes occur, a public deviant may be created. At the very least, exclusion rituals will be set in motion and a moratorium may be established. A "trial period" of conduct will be set up and the potential deviant is then given a set period of time to prove himself worthy of relational membership.

A third condition for the relational threat arises when the rules of conduct begin to undergo change within the relationship. One of the members may adopt a new perspective and begin acting on what to the other members appears as unreasonable and unacceptable grounds. One occasion reported to the author involved the introduction of certain illicit drugs in a marriage that had long sanctioned the excessive use of alcohol for purposes of relational-release. The wife refused to accept this new definition and the husband refused to change his line of action. Collective behavior within the relationship occurred and lasted until a compromise was established.

In this situation, the wife felt the morality of her relationship was being threatened because the conduct of her husband under the influence of drugs was unlike anything he theretofore had engaged in. The introduction of new perspectives and new lines of action can potentially threaten the stability of any relationship. It is important to keep in mind that these transgressions carry greater implications for the relationship than do the momentary acts of embarrassment discussed earlier.

Relational Morality and the Broader Social Order

Having discussed the circumstances under which varying degrees of relational impropriety are sensed, I now turn to the connection between relational moralities and perceptions of deviance by the broader social order. I now move away from the forms of deviance and misconduct that never come to the public's eye. Involvement in a relational social structure can lead to varying reactions by members of society's social control agencies. I am dealing, then, with situations where public deviance is either ascribed to a relational member or is rechanneled back into the relationship.

ASCRIPTIONS OF PUBLIC DEVIANCE

Speaking abstractly, it may be hypothesized that the greater the involvement in a relational social structure, the lower the probability of deviance ascription by members of social control agencies. That is, labeling will not occur if the potential deviant is highly involved in a relational network. Several contingency factors must be noted. First, the degree of societal legitimacy and power attributed to the offender and his relationship, must be considered (Scheff, 1963, pp. 436–53). Under conditions of high power and high legitimacy the lowest rates of public deviance would be predicted. This hyothesis is supported by research in the areas of both delinquency and mental illness. Kitsuse and Cicourel have shown that in an upper-class Chicago suburb acts of delinquency were written off as routine conduct among the youth of that area (Kitsuse and Cicourel, 1963, pp. 135–39; Cicourel, 1968). The typical approbation given by the chief of police was that "good kids don't get in trouble." In lower-class areas just the reverse occurred. When rates of publicly diagnosed and treated mental illness are considered, the classic findings of Hollingshead and Redlich indicate similar conclusions. The higher the social class of the potential deviant, the lower the rates of publicly ascribed mental illness (Hollingshead and Redlich, 1958).

Similar processes operate under conditions of high political influence but relatively low social status. Thus members of powerful street gangs are less likely to be booked and charged for delinquent offenses than are members of less prestigious and powerful gangs (Thrasher, 1963; Landesco, 1964; Vold, 1958).

These data suggest that sociologists may most profitably view any social structure as a complex arrangement of varying moral orders and relational statuses. Those persons bound into powerful relational structures can expect relative immunity in the face of public deviance, while those lower in the moral hierarchy may be penalized for the very actions that found their source in the persons above them.

Under other conditions ascriptions of public deviance are observable but to a lesser degree, because the deviant is involved in a relationship. Thus Bittner (1967a, pp. 669–715; 1967b, pp. 278–92) shows that police in skid row areas are less likely to pick up and charge a law violator if he can show relational membership in an occupational or family structure. Similarly, once booked and treated by a social control agency, the deviant remains in that status in a time inversely proportional to the strength and prestige of his ongoing relational structures. Thus mental patients are more likely to be released soon after admission if they can show relational need and if pressure from their relationships can be made public. Under conditions of no or little involvement in a relational structure, we can predict a much longer hospitalization, incarceration, or treatment. (See Simmons, Davis, Spencer, 1956, pp. 21–28.)

As a person moves through his life cycle there will be varying moments of high and low public deviancy potential. In fact, the structure of our society's social control and treatment agencies directly corresponds to variations in the life cycle. These arrangements reflect an implicit belief that one's relational involvements vary by his age. Thus, with great deal of ease and relative immunity we can place our aged in retirement homes, our retarded in special institutions, and our juveniles in detention homes.

THE COMMUNICATION OF RELATIONAL IMPROPRIETY
TO AGENCIES OF SOCIAL CONTROL

The statements above suggest a number of conditions under which one's relational status at the moment affects his perceptions by agencies of social control. I wish to examine now those conditions where members of relational structures bring into the public's eye a case of deviance.

Earlier, I suggested several conditions that give rise to a sense of self- or relational threat. These same dimensions can be pursued one step further. As the relational deviance exceeds the tolerance limits of the involved members the probability of exposing it to the outside increases. Hence, when embarrassing acts persist and increase in regularity, it may become apparent to relational members that they no longer can control the deviant. When a relational act remains confined to the relationship, public denouncement is less likely than if it recurrently comes to the eye of other friends and acquaintances. All people can handle deviance at home, but when it occurs publicly it causes embarrassment to the entire relationship. And relationships, I have suggested, can tolerate only a certain degree of public embarrassment.

Intrusions by third parties can bring in new perspectives and also disrupt the accommodation that has evolved between the potential public deviant and his relational partners. Sampson, Messinger, and Towne (1962, pp. 88–96) suggest that the intrusion of mother-in-law into husband-wife dyad brought a wife's deviant acts out into the open and led to hospitalization. This would seem to be a special case of bringing a new perspective or line of action into the relationship (Ichheiser, 1949).

On occasion relational partners will deliberately stage situations so that one of the members can be formally and legitimately excluded. These occasions are best represented in acts of betrayal, which Goffman (1961a, pp. 131–46) has shown to operate in certain phases of the mental patient's moral career. Betraying another relational partner seems to represent the extreme point of termination for the relationship. The betrayer has shifted his alliances to another moral order and is now searching for a convenient and socially acceptable exit from his present relationship. Thus, actions that formerly were accommodated and accepted begin to be viewed in another light and the betrayer begins to evoke a morality that would not sanction such actions. The *betrayed* soon finds himself in the uncomfortable position of no longer having the self and relational support he formerly expected from his partner. For an act of betrayal to be successfully carried off, the betrayed must not know why he is being excluded and who the actual betrayer is (Goffman, 1961a, pp. 482–505). Thus, as Goffman suggests, third parties in the form of relatives, members from social control agencies, and friends will be brought in to bear the brunt of the responsibility. The strategy for this action is clear: no moral responsibility can be placed in the betrayer, and the betrayed can now be shown to be morally incompetent and hence no longer deserving or fit to be a member of his focal relationship. He becomes the perfect mark, to be cooled out by our agencies of social control. Of course once he has been shown to be morally unfit, all responsibility for maintaining the former relationship is removed from the betrayer. He or she is now free to enter into any other relationship. Thus, having dispensed with a burdensome and troublesome partner a new life in another moral order can be begun. To summarize, I am suggesting that in the case of betrayal, the betrayer assigns the label of public deviant as a convenient means of terminating the relationship. In some situations a member of a relationship deliberately seeks out a label of public deviance. This is most frequently the case in voluntary admissions to mental hospitals. The prepatient comes to view his own actions as deviant and no longer morally acceptable, to himself or his relational mates. Under these circumstances amicable resolutions are made, with both partners agreeing that it is the proper and correct line of action. The relationship is thus not terminated, but only held in abeyance for the duration of treatment or incarceration. When this occurs the relationship's role in its relational social structure is likely to go unthreatened. Friends will feel that the partners took the proper action, and no lasting aspersions are cast on the relationship's overall legitimacy and morality.

These are all instances when the matter of relational deviance rises out of the relationship and comes to the public's eye. On these occasions the fragile morality of the relationship is most severely tested. Depending on the degree of commitment and involvement held by the relational members, these social orders may either dissolve and disappear or take on renewed strength and vigor as a result of the publicity they have received. The relational responses to such instances also vary by the nature of the public label and public reaction. Hence, in cases of relational impropriety I predict lower rates of dissolution than when one of the relational partners commits an action that challenges the legal and moral order of his broader society. In short, if the public reaction is primarily limited to a relational social structure (e.g., a character flaw indicative of mental illness), milder forms of exclusion and lower rates of relational collapse occur than if the action comes to the attention of an entire community, organization, or work group.

Friendship as a
Social Institution

In the context of one specific type of social relationship,
friendship, rules of propriety are in this essay shown to be
simply and distinctively transformed within relationships; the
role of these transformed proprieties in initiating and maintaining such intimate relationships is carefully explored. The
personal and social functions of the transformed morality of
friendship (including, again, the insulation of deviance) are
so great as to foster the *institutionalization* of friendship.
Relations with other institutions and organizations—particularly the "bridging function" of friendship—are examined in
this light.

Friendship choices and the attraction among individuals are
heavily explored topics in American sociology (Burgess and
Wallen, 1943; Newcomb, 1961). We know that people tend to like
one another when they have similar statuses, attractive attributes,
ample access to one another, and meet often. We know far less
about friendship as a social institution that fits into the general
pattern of total societies and fulfills certain social functions. This

is a tentative attempt to look into the question of why friendship as a social institution should exist at all and why American sociologists have rightly been so concerned with friendship choices.

If we look at friendship as a social institution, some of its functions seem almost immediately apparent. Friendships are especially valued in a population where social contacts have outgrown the bounds of kinship, neighborhood, age grades, work groups, ethnicity, and social classes. Most modern societies are, to stretch a term used by Service (1962, p. 59–99) composite societies, where many people are unrelated by primordial ties (Shils, 1957, pp. 30–45; Geertz, 1963, pp. 105–57) or a division of labor that joins everyone into a single authority structure. Some broad and flexible covenant that joins people to one another and regulates their interpersonal relations is obviously needed. Friendship, then, fills in where the more mechanical and exclusionary institutions fail to define interpersonal affiliations.

Friendship, of course, is not unique to modern industrial and composite societies (Firth, 1936). It is probably universal, although especially prominent in industrialized societies where immigration and migration have contributed heavily to population composition.[1] In all societies, however, friendship seems to serve the same end by allowing people to go beyond institutionally required affiliations. In some societies, kinship societies for instance, ascriptive institutional provisions include practically every social relationship. In other societies, generally the more modern and transient ones, a vast proportion, perhaps most, of all social relations are not included within a single institution. Thus, while friendship is probably universal, its relative frequency points up the way friendship allows people to go beyond the basic framework of their institutions and affiliate themselves with persons in relatively distinct institutions.

1. Despite the prevalence of the "equivalence of alternate generations" it is unlikely that people would report such relations as "friendships." Since these relations are institutionally prescribed, however, we should expect as much because friendship is defined as a voluntaristic relationship. Indeed, the failure to report close affective ties across alternative generations points up the importance of voluntaristic considerations in the definition of friendship.

This functional chore of friendship is evident in the cultural features that go into its definition. First, friendship is a very generalized relationship and can occur within strata or existing groups as well as between them. Coworkers can become friends and supplement or confirm already existing relations. Conversely, people belonging to quite different groupings can and do become friends to link discrete institutions and populations. Moreover, the generalized character of friendship creates a note of equality, which enjoins those in the same or different institutions to moderate their differences; friendship, then, has a leveling influence not only among friends but among all others drawn together within the same congregation. The friends of friends are required to treat each other as equals.

Second, friendship is usually regarded as a voluntaristic and intensely personal relation. Friendship is perceived directly as a means of going beyond prescribed institutional or organizational affiliations. It seems safe to say that even in the eyes of those who join in friendship, it is regarded as an interstitial institution to bridge the chasm between groups, organizations, populations, and social categories.

Third, friendships are subject to private negotiation to an extent unparallelled in most other social relations. Persons may break their friendship, revise it, or simply drift away from one another without notifying anyone else. Losing a friend may be painful but it is also an option that can be taken without consultation or an official change in status; being an ex-friend is not a publicly recognized status, as is so often the case when a person severs any other type of affiliation.

The importance of these three defining elements of the institution of friendship can be brought into relief by comparing friendship to other forms of affiliation; marriage, business partnerships, godparenthood, and so on. Marriage, for example, can relate only people of the opposite sex. Marriage makes in-laws but not equals of the kinfolk of the bride and groom. Similarly, a marriage cannot be dissolved without the intervention of a third party or a change in the status of marital partners. Husbands and wives do not simply separate; they become divorcees, widows, or widowers. Friendships, on the other hand, can be revised, broken and/or put in abeyance without necessarily changing the status of people or drawing in the judgment of a third party.

Doubtless friendship has its limits. Very few elderly people would claim that their best friend is an infant or child. In general the frequency of friendships follows a pattern marked out by other forms of affiliation. People who are similar in status, belong to the same groups, and share the same values get married, join in business partnerships, and become friends. But while all other forms of affiliation have discrete limits, friendship is always possible even between the most disparate groups. In this sense friendship is similar to other forms of social affiliation but it is broader in scope and for that reason more important as an interstitial institution.

Since friendship seems to serve primarily as an interstitial institution, one can go on to suggest three lines of inquiry on how the institution operates. First, since friendship is not a prescribed relationship, there is the question of how cultural and situational elements combine so that people can decipher the inception and course of their friendships. Second, there is the problem of how institutional safeguards work with more or less effect to restrict the growth of friendships. Finally, there is the small private culture of friendship itself, with its own internal order and special content. These general areas establish the rough metes and bounds of this paper.

The Cultural and Situational Elements of Friendship

THE CONCEPT OF FRIENDSHIP

When persons say that they are friends, usually they can point to cultural images, rules of conduct, and customary modes of behavior to confirm their claims. This is likely to be most apparent when one or both parties find their relationship questioned by outsiders. At these times there will be an appeal to standards, rules, or "facts" by which persons can validate whether or not they are, indeed, "friends." Although there may be a good deal of individual variation in this respect, in broad perspective the concept of friendship seems to involve at least the following considerations.

1. The other person in the relationship is positively evaluated as a person *qua* person rather than for incidental advantages that may accrue as a result of an encounter with him. Thus, it is said to be inappropriate or "insincere" if one's liking of another is contingent upon advantages other than those intrinsic to an appreciation of the person himself. Consequently, any note of utilitarianism or hint of self-interest is felt to discredit a relationship founded upon "true friendship."

2. It is appropriate to appreciate the objective qualities, private property, or social characteristics of a friend only because they represent the person himself rather than for any universal value attached to them. To like a person because of his money, his hair, his eyes, or other physical attractions is not to like the person but only those embellishments attached to him. Instead, one is to appreciate these artifacts only in their capacity to symbolize the other person quite aside from any general merit they may have of their own. To suggest that one's friendship with another would end if he lost his money, good looks, or social standing is usually felt to disclose one's affections as fraudulent. But more than this, it also means that one cannot like another because of his public "face," "façade" or "front." Thus, the person liked must be regarded as a "real self" apart from all pretense.

3. Exchanges between friends must not be evaluated in terms of their appeal to the general public, their "market value," but only in reference to what are considered to be the individual tastes, needs, and preferences of the other's real self. Hence it is inappropriate to express friendship by making a gift that is not of value to the other's real self irrespective of the general value placed on the gift. The man who brings his hospitalized friend the monetary equivalent of a vase of flowers will generally be thought odd or even coarse.

Any transfer meant to express friendship must take into consideration what are judged to be the other's particular tastes, preferences, or needs. Money or other economic goods are appropriate gifts only if they coincide with the particular needs assumed on behalf of the person's real self. In this sense exchanges between friends must be regarded as expressions of approval of their respective real selves. In turn, any expression of regard for the other's real self must be "given freely" without hope of any return other than the continuity of the other's real self. If returns are expected, then it is because this form of reciprocity is implicitly assumed to be characteristic of the other's real self. A failure of a friend to observe reciprocity may be taken as an indication of a change in his real self, but not as a failure to "repay" one for services previously rendered. In this case, one might justifiably sever relations with a friend who fails to recompense one's demonstrations of liking only because there is an apparent change in his real self rather than a loss of service or goods valued in their own right. If, perchance, a person were liked specifically on the grounds that he never observed reciprocity, then a failure on his part to do so would hardly be the basis for severing the relationship.

4. The person who is a friend must be appreciated as a unique self rather than simply a particular instance of a general class. To suggest that a friend could be adequately or arbitrarily replaced by someone else who meets the same general criteria is usually felt to be antithetical to "true friendship." To abandon a person because one has found another "just as good" is usually considered to be both hypocritical and an admission of self-interest. To like another only as a representative of a type is to like the type rather than the person *qua* person. Friendship then, inevitably means being attached to someone as a specific, unique self.

THE SITUATIONAL ELEMENTS OF FRIENDSHIP

If individuals are going to engage themselves in friendship, the first assumption they must be able to make is that they have grounds for believing that each is presenting a "real self." Otherwise there can be no appreciation of the other *qua* person, but only as a "face," a "façade," "role," or "front." So long as interaction does not penetrate beyond these boundaries, individuals remain at a distance, unable to claim friendship because they will feel they cannot detect the person behind the actor.[2]

This means that there must be some test or demonstration of individuality or sincerity. On the one hand, this test must single

2. For somewhat different reasons Erving Goffman (1963b) has made the same distinction between one's real self and social self.

out the individual as someone distinct from other people who occupy the same role or social status. On the other hand, such tests must contrast the person's behavior against what seems expedient, conventional, or merely routine. There are, I suggest, essentially three ways an individual can display such a "real self." The first is by violating public propriety and contrasting one's own self-presentation with what is conventional or routine. The second consists of collective remissions from public propriety, such as those witnessed in saturnalia at one extreme and cocktail parties at the other extreme. Finally, there are those many social situations that simply jostle people together into an involuntary and uncontrollable exposure of self.

Individual Violations of Public Propriety. There are many situations in which an individual should always put his best foot forward. Ceremonial occasions are perhaps the most extreme of this type. Such occasions are highly conventionalized and the behavior of participants governed by a detailed set of rules. Taken together these rules constitute a large part of what is called "public propriety." Broadly speaking these rules of propriety represent safe patterns of behavior that can be enacted before the widest possible audience without exciting justifiable ridicule or criticism.[3]

When public propriety is well observed, it subdues controversy, dissension, or conflict (Toby, 1952). In a self-conscious way people follow a scenario acknowledged to be separate or independent from their individual inclinations. Ordinarily it will be necessary to disattend any gross or striking displays of individuality so long as they do not become completely disruptive. Concomitantly, there is the obligation to disregard past grievances or present misgivings that might interrupt the passage of this practiced order. Action is supposed to move along in smooth steps in a predictable sequence without calling into question the motives, roles, or honor of anyone.

---

3. I have used here the word "propriety" because it seems the most generic among those that refer to rules that are only conventional: e.g., good manners, civility, discretion, etiquette, and politeness. Each of these latter terms has its own special connotation but is still included in Webster's (1955) definition of propriety, "Conformity with accepted standards of manners or behavior." Needless to say, I am concerned to maintain the colloquial or proper meaning of the term.

Conduct in keeping with public propriety is most evident in ceremonial or formal situations. Church services, high school graduations, and court proceedings, for example, are heavily dependent upon the rules of public propriety. But the rules of public propriety are widely scattered through different realms of life. In almost all large congregations of people, except for mobs and panics, the rules of public propriety are brought into play. Such rules are also likely to be invoked among strangers and especially at the introduction of strangers.

On the whole the rules of public propriety seem to be most concentrated in those social gatherings where people lack much foreknowledge of each others' intentions or are subject to wide and unknown divisions. The high point of public propriety probably occurs in diplomatic circles where the rules of propriety become particularly impressive in negotiations on sensitive issues such as a war or boundary settlement. Indeed, being "diplomatic" is a generalized way of saying that a person is closely attending the rules of propriety so as to evade any direct reference to personal or social differences. Typically, one is also "diplomatic" in interracial gatherings, in cross-sex groups, in a foreign country, or among one's elders.

The great value of the rules of propriety is that they make life safe by muting all or most sources of individual or social dissension. This muting is achieved simply, through everyone following a code itself regarded as sufficiently distinct from individual or group preference to assure people of their safety. Here the language for describing very proper relations is quite clear. Very proper relations are said to be "stiff," to lack spontaneity, to be "just so much motion," and to be unrelaxed.

Because the rules of propriety are so obviously distinct or independent of individual preference, these rules also form a remarkably good benchmark against which individuality can be identified and assessed. Deviations—almost any deviation—from the rules of propriety when they are in force leave us with the impression that someone has behaved out of choice. Such actions are almost invariably attributed to something basic and essential to the individual; a sort of unalterable and irrepressible force.

In part, deviations from public propriety are taken to betray individuality simply because they are departures from the routine.

What gives these exemplars of individuality credibility, however, is their general tendency to abandon expediency and safety. The rules of propriety make life safe for people in situations fraught with the dangers of conflict, attack, and embarrassment. The person who violates these rules takes grave risks and shows in doing so that there is some portion of himself so irrepressible that it cannot be bribed or forced into compliance. This adds greatly to the view that violations of public propriety betray a sort of bedrock reality in individual character. Now, we say, we know "what he's really like" because he "hasn't been able to contain himself." It is not that the individual has lost self-control, but he has signaled some portion of himself not susceptible to social control.

Of course, these judgments on what signals a person's "real self" may be entirely wrong. It is altogether possible that some people find the rules of propriety so entirely to their liking that they embrace them with spontaneity and enthusiasm. It is also possible that some violations of public propriety are entirely incidental to a person's own views of himself; they may be due to sheer mechanical failures on the part of his body or speech organs. This, however, will not change much the judgmental process that people exercise upon each other's behavior and the inferences they draw from it. Thus the person who denies he "meant" to violate some rule of propriety may be humored and excused—propriety demands this response as well—but it need not change people's views on what he is "really like."[4] Indeed, it might be argued that the individual himself must take such improprieties and somehow incorporate them into his own private concept of self.

Deviations from public propriety can go in two rather obvious and opposite directions. On the one hand, a person may fall short of public propriety by becoming vulgar, outspoken, or irreverent. Faux pas, boners, and gaffes are small ways we simply indicate our ineptitude at maintaining propriety. Laughing at a funeral, making sexual overtures during church, or refusing to shake someone's hand are taken as baser threats to public propriety. Im-

---

4. Especially in the post-Freudian revolution, when slips of the tongue may be regarded as exceptionally strong evidence of one's most deep-rooted tendencies. One consequence of the Freudian revolution has been to make "slips" of behavior the most eloquent and direct index to one's "real self."

proprieties of this sort suggest a less exacting social order where discipline and social control are simply disregarded.

On the other hand, it is equally possible for an individual to exceed the rules of social propriety by becoming overly idealistic, straightlaced or simply by overdoing it. If someone can cry too little at a funeral, someone else may cry too much. And while some people eat, drink, talk, and laugh too much, others may participate so little as to suggest that the present social order is far too lax and undemanding.

Either way of going against the grain of public propriety is equally able to furnish people with a real self they must live with afterward. Perhaps this is one reason why those argot terms that indicate an individual identity, rather than a social role, so often come in pairs, each the opposite of the other. For the deadbeat there is the mark, for the drunk there is the teetotaler, and for the prude the make-out artist. But this division into opposites also grows out of a much larger cultural system, including our language itself. Adjectives ordinarily come in pairs, each of them indicating some extreme from a common base. Similarly, real selves must be placed somewhere off center and, like the adjectives describing them, diverge in opposite directions.

Not all people are equally subject to all the rules of propriety. Children, for example, may defecate, scream, cry, or slobber with relative impunity. There is not much a very young child can do to violate public propriety and thus not much in the way of a real self that others can attribute to him. There are, of course, limits. The child who cries practically all the time is unusual, as is the child who is exceptionally quiet and amenable. While the limits of propriety are stretched very wide for infants, they do not include everything. Some of these extremes of infant behavior are remembered, usually by the parent rather than the child, and used to attribute a rudimentary real self to the child. But on the whole the limits of propriety are so wide for children that they do provide a moratorium and allow us to think that children do not have "much personality."

With advancing age the limits of public propriety usually narrow, and the opportunities to acquire a real self are enriched. At this point, however, the opportunity for obeying or disobeying public propriety are likely to diverge somewhat according to one's social class, religion, ethnicity, or community. Jewish children with traditional parents must somehow get through bar mitzvah while Catholic children have to take fewer risks in a group confirmation. Among storefront gypsies, the rules of propriety seem bifurcated between what are significant violations before members of one's own ethnic group and before outsiders. Members of the family may dress, eat, work, and sleep in full view of other ethnic groups but still observe a fairly strict level of propriety among themselves. In this way, perhaps, the storefront gypsy's real self is rooted firmly in the opinions of his own ethnic group, while with other ethnic groups he enjoys an eternal moratorium.

In general, the lower classes enjoy much greater freedom from the rules of public propriety and have a harder time announcing their individuality. As with children, a great deal is tolerated on the part of the lower classes, and while they frequently violate respectable notions of public propriety, not much of it is attributed to them as individuals. On the one hand, it is frequently observed that one reason they are lower class is because they do not know about the rules of propriety. On the other hand, members of the lower classes are seldom involved in highly formal circumstances or called upon to act as representatives of large and prestigeful groups who have much to lose by their improprieties. Thus, lower-class individuals must try harder to show that they have some individual proclivities that go beyond the wide boundaries of propriety permitted to them as a group. Judging from available studies they do indeed try harder and succeed in differentiating themselves into two camps; those after a "rep" and those frightfully conventional (Gans, 1962, pp. 28–31; Miller, 1958).

The rules of propriety bear most heavily upon those who occupy high government office, speak and act in public places, and represent large and prestigeful associations. For such persons the limits of public propriety are very narrow and frequently encountered. Any misstep or miscue will surely be recorded and add to that list of credits and demerits that allows them a "real self." This leads to something of a paradox, for it is often those who are most subject to the heavy hand of public propriety who also can be singled out as having the most distinctive and incontrovertible "real selves." Probably the most excessive example of this type are movie stars whose every move is public and the source of constant diagnosis for a real self. Inevitably movie stars fail to live up to the full epitome of public propriety and acquire a rich image of self, which is considered both real and irrefutable. In turn, movie stars can go far against the rules of public propriety but find their own precedent harder to deny. Of course there are also options here. Ingrid Bergman arouses a storm of protest if she divorces her husband. Elizabeth Taylor must change husbands, or at least lovers, with some regularity to keep her billing. In public life, the simple rules of propriety are often less important than those established by known precedent.

Violations of public propriety do not alone make for friendship. They do, however, single the individual out and make known his real self sufficiently well to where others can tell if he is even eligible for friendship. Ordinarily, of course, friendship is the exception rather than the rule—but this is true of all social contacts. Violations of public propriety are offensive by and large because they suggest that people will not look after each other's public character with great care or circumspection. Generally, but not invariably, this is so. As an individual diverges off the sure path of propriety he is apt to run into kindred souls who have previously been derailed in the same direction. Between such individuals can develop a fellow feeling not based upon a common set of norms and values but a shared attitude expressed toward norms and values.

Of course, occasions where the rules of propriety are strongly enforced are a bad place to begin friendships. Violations of public propriety, then, must work their way into social relations indirectly or as a sort of aftermath. Once away from the scene of their improprieties, coparticipants can celebrate their outrages like school boys who lose all their contriteness when they are off the school grounds. Such periods are often the occasion for euphoria and certitude, because not only has a person's character been tested but proven.

Even solo violations of propriety seem to work their way into friendships. Every friendship circle seems to have its inventory of stories about how its members have been "horribly embarrassed" or expressed their feelings "despite all." Outrageous drunks, contesting the judgment of a policeman, or refusing to "be quiet" in public circumstances are all grist for the mill among friends. These little stories are told and retold among friends, for they are among the most dramatic milestones that people have to verify the reality of their selves. People who do not have such experiences to recount may be obliged to invent them. Others will be tempted to enlarge upon what would otherwise be bona fide violations of public propriety. In any event, friendship demands a verifiable self and it cannot be one that complacently complies with public propriety.

Collective Remissions from Public Propriety. At the other extreme from situations demanding great propriety are a series of situations where people are collectively exempted from many of the rules of propriety. The best examples of this type are orgies, stag parties, saturnalia, festspeilen, and masked balls. Cocktail parties, coffee klatches, smokers, and the ordinary house party represent more partial attempts to relieve people from public propriety. At these social gatherings the individual finds it not only possible but obligatory to violate at least a few rules of public propriety. Here again the natural language is rich in allusions that make clear the relationship between self and society. At such occasions a person must "let down his hair," "feel free," "swing" or simply "go, go, go!" Certainly one must avoid being a "party pooper," "deadhead," "wet blanket," "killjoy," or just plain "square." What is required is that each person disclose something about himself that would be embarrassing or damaging in a less restricted audience. Ordinarily this means a suggestive rather than a fully deviant action; thus, except for orgies, only the rules of public propriety are violated.

The obligation to disclose some damaging or embarrassing information about oneself serves here the same function as that disclosed in very proper circumstances. Such information is testimony to the bedrock self assumed to lie "beyond the façade" of contrivance or even the necessity for contrivance. Individuals are called upon to show themselves, and there can be no failure to pass this test. Collective remissions from public propriety are merciless in their subsequent judgments. There can be no excuse for maintaining public propriety in these collective remissions, and however one behaves, he is equally accountable. The "party pooper" who draws back, the "square" who always treads a safe course, and the "life of the party" are all real selves that get distilled out of such remissions from public propriety.

Since these collective remissions from public propriety always test for individuality, they can be especially trying and difficult for people who find themselves well attuned to the ordinary conventions of public propriety. At some point such people must be urged or cajoled to disclose a slightly improper self despite their own misgivings. A particularly interesting example of this are "party games," which seem to have as an essential ingredient some requirement that the participants confess some failing or excess that, no matter how atypical, is taken as diagnostic of their "real self." Perhaps the most blatant of these party games is that constructed by Dostovesky in *The Idiot,* where the participants must confess absolutely the most horrible thing they have ever done. By contrast, "spin the bottle" is a relatively harmless exercise.

Each of these collective remissions from public propriety seem somewhat distinct, especially in their phasing and what they aim to disclose. Orgies are particularly different because they require people to do what they say they would do. Stag parties and smokers are only suggestive, although what they frequently suggest is an orgy. Saturnalia and festspeilen often take long periods of time to complete and allow role reversals that call upon people to attack existing status differences and the propriety they impose. Masked balls make everyone an impostor for a time but require him to unmask at the end. The cocktail party is an especially interesting case because it starts with a studied display of public propriety and gradually declines in its standards of what is admissible behavior. Many other remissions from public propriety allow the maximum of license in their earlier phases and only later draw in the reins of accountability. Perhaps it is this reversal of phasing that makes the cocktail party particularly subject to the allegation of "phoniness."

Despite their internal variation, however, all these collective remissions from public propriety allow a reading on what seems the more inalterable and irrefutable portions of an individual's self. These remissions from public propriety lay the underpinnings for a new type of moral order composed of the values expressed by individuals rather than families, communities, or nations. This private morality is the first step toward giving a friendship its shape and in singling it out from other relations. In this sense, friends are a little like partners in crime; it is their expressed views of society and not society alone that binds them together.

These remissions from public propriety may vary a great deal in the distinctness of the boundaries that separate them from the remaining society. A saturnalia, mardi gras, or festspeilen include the total community but are sharply marked off acording to when they begin or end. Cocktail parties, orgies, smokers, and house parties are "by invitation only" and much more restricted to people who already know one another. Fiestas, promenades, and roadhouses have a more transient membership where the categories of age, sex, and income are the major principles of segregation. Each type of remission from public propriety presents a somewhat different opportunity structure for personal disclosures. Traditional saturnalia involve the whole community and juxtapose persons of very different social rank. House parties, smokers, and cocktail parties pair people who are very similar in social rank but need not share any common residential unit.

It is at least an attractive hypothesis that the membership boundaries for the dominant type of collective remission from public propriety meets a particular integragtive problem in the society within which it occurs. In a relatively isolated local community the major divisions may be those among the social ranks juxtaposed in saturnalia. In a region of competing communities, roadhouses and fiestas may act as a common meeting ground for competitors. In modern societies, which are highly mobile and transient, the main problem may be to bring together age, sex, and interest groups widely separated or constantly rearranged in space. Thus, the invitational party, under the supervision of a sensitive host, is a primary instrument for creating "togetherness" where it is most absent.

Whatever the society, people differ in their opportunity to participate in these collective remissions from public propriety. Some people get invited to practically everything and some to none. In modern industrial societies, the professional and business classes tend to have many sharply distinct social gatherings where they can go and violate public propriety. On their own part, the lowest strata of these industrial societies can shamelessly turn their streets and even their work place into a sort of bacchanalia (Roy, 1959–60). It is the aged, divorced, and ugly who find themselves without a stage on which to parade even their shortcomings (Edgerton, 1967). And it is from these groups that one often hears a resigned wail of loneliness and abandon.

It is the explicit aim of these collective remissions from public propriety to allow people to form friendships or at least acquaintances. Doubtless such gatherings are usually successful and in recent years commercial firms have even gone into the business of helping people "let down their hair" and violate public propriety. For example, the "T-group technique" and "office party" are calculated attempts to engender a private morality among employees. Welcome wagons and the professional community organizer seem to be ways whole communities have subcontracted their responsibility to make people "feel at home." Even the churches have recently gone into the business of providing "sensitivity training" and "nonverbal" experiences meant to free people from their inhibitions (O'Conner, 1963).

One can applaud the intent of these efforts without being too hopeful about their results. The central assumption friends must make is that they are presenting a self free of contrivance and ulterior motives. The commercial programming of self-disclosure, however, tends to provide only another social scenario that can be studied, practiced, and performed. Thus, no matter how spontaneous and crude a person's expressed self, there is a shade of doubt about his reality. Such contrived remissions from public propriety may be the scene of great license, but I suspect that the participants find it hard to transfer their newfound real selves to other situations.

Involuntary Violations of Public Propriety. The rules of public propriety can be brought into play only where technological, ecological, and chronological arrangements allow people to separate front and back regions. Public propriety demands that people keep out of view those things and activities that are emblematic of their personal differences and represent universal shortcomings. If a person is to avoid showing his genitals to others, then he must have a private place to urinate. If a woman wants to appear "years younger" she must not be seen putting on her girdle. If husbands and wives are to have intercourse without the knowledge of their children, then bedrooms and sleeping times must be carefully arranged.

Temporal scheduling and ecological segregation are the main ways all societies provide for some degree of privacy and protect the rules of propriety from continual violation. In modern societies, technological innovations have considerably advanced both the level of privacy and the partiality of the view people can have of one another. The telephone, for example, allows people to maintain a very proper conversation while their appearance, surroundings, and gestures are totally improper. Invitations would be scarcely possible without the modern postal service, which permits a housewife to have her best foot forward when guests appear.

Obviously, however, there are many circumstances where an individual can no longer clothe himself in privacy or hide many of his imperfections. In a prison, for example, inmates find that their keepers have the right to inquire into their sex life, toilet training, and privy parts. These inmates also find that they must dress, urinate, defecate, sleep, masturbate, and bathe before the same people as they may try to impress with their "propriety." This requirement is true generally of "total institutions," such as mental hospitals and the armed services (Goffman, 1961a, pp. 1–124). As Goffman points out, people are "mortified" at the prospect of being unable to keep separate their real and social selves. The contradictions are so great and the collision between these different sectors of life so sharp that individuals sometimes simply give up all their claims to a social order "higher" than their own appetites. Life becomes gross, vulgar, shameless, and crude.

As Goffman observes, this almost complete lapse from the rules of propriety is typical of total institutions. People must and do pick their noses, dress, and perform all of their bodily functions in a common social setting. Arguing, "looking out for number one," and blatant references to social interest groups ("niggers," "politicians," etc.) demonstrate clearly how the inability to maintain public propriety opens numerous sources of conflict (Skyes, 1958). Yet one can agree with Goffman's observations, without going further to conclude that life among the inmates of a total institution is just disorganized. Rather, the general trend seems to be toward a "lopsided" social organization in which informal relations far outweigh the importance of enduring social roles. In this rather simple network of personal relations, friendship of some form seems to be the most positive force that gives people a basis for their sense of personal safety and mutual cooperation (Little, 1964). The moral guidelines for such associations, however, are those struck up by individuals rather than those provided at the outset by social organization. In turn, individual identities often replace social identities to define those aspects of social life "you can really depend on." Concurrently, there is the development of a vast range of argot terms that transform slightly or very much the social world portrayed in "proper English" (Kantrowitz).

Indeed, judging from Wentworth and Flexner, practically all our argot or slang terms originate in total institutions or in populations similarly unable to keep separate front and back regions (Wentworth and Flexner, 1960). Hobos and tramps, for instance, start without much claim to the rules of propriety and a communal pattern of eating, sleeping, drinking, bathing, and "mooching," which further erodes any claims they have made. Jazz musicians, baseball players, and show business people must contend with a travel "circuit" and congested quarters for dressing, eating, and sleeping, which cast people of very different status together in very intimate circumstances (Kiel, 1966, pp. 143–63). Here the role of public performer is especially interesting because the distinction between front stage and back stage does not just identify different aspects of an individual, but different social worlds as well. On stage, public performers as well as their audience follow a scenario that clearly exists apart from their individual impulses or designs. Backstage, however, the leading man does not retreat to regal privacy but is cast among half-dressed chorus girls, sweaty workmen, stage door johnnies, and enraged stage directors. Familiarity and the tokens of friendship violently trespass upon status differences and the rules of public propriety. What one sees enacted is not just a release from a "required self" but a sudden engagement into a new social order as unbalanced toward informality as that on stage is unbalanced toward formality.

Certain residential groupings can also render people ineffective at maintaining "appearances" and force their members into a lopsided social order of friendship and personal enmities. Dormitory living quarters among college students, migrant workers, and lumberjacks seem to have this consequence (Lofland, 1968). A less obvious example is households where crowding and the absence of certain facilities (private bedrooms, bathrooms, and play spaces) throw together family quarrels, lovemaking, and dressing to such an extent that kinsmen can no longer pretend that they are the epitome of propriety (Schorr, 1963).

Most often these crowded family living quarters are concentrated near one another and are especially likely to be occupied by persons from a low status ethnic or income group. Intrafamilial disclosures, then, are not likely to be isolated events, but like all information work their way outward to an eager and understanding audience. Thus, family skeletons are allowed to roam out of their closets and given reign among a circle of coresidents who are both sympathetic and perhaps a little eager to find fault in their neighbors (Suttles, 1968, pp. 72–98).

Such residential groups give rise to a private morality based on a particular existential perspective about what people are "really like," rather than ideal values and a neat ecological or temporal separation between behavior carried out in public or private (Rainwater, 1966). Sociologists have drawn from these observations the notion of a subculture or contraculture, but this is at best an unfair or inaccurate representation (Singer, 1960). Groups who have failed to present themselves in the best light must look for some other way of presenting themselves to one another. For these groups the rules of public propriety no longer obtain, at least in full force. In deciding upon what sort of second-order morality they can sustain, the rules of friendship and personal negotiation form a more durable and credible basis for wending one's way among other people.

One cannot review all of these examples without observing that there are gradations in the way groups move away from public propriety, and that distinctive patterns hold for each gradation. At one extreme are the armed services, which violate many of the ecological and temporal conditions conducive to a proper presentation of self, but nonetheless provide a counter balancing arena for public propriety. Service men go on parades, are subject to strict inspections, and constantly forewarned that they must keep their uniform and gear in order. For servicemen, rather contrived displays of public propriety always offset their own tendency into a private morality distinguished only by friendship, personal enmities, and a negotiated order. Indeed, it might be argued that the armed services achieve a sort of optimum balance between formal and informal social orders so that either one can take over wherever the other is unmanned either by death or confusion— both frequent circumstances on the battlefield (Shils and Janowitz, 1948).

Even in prisons and boarding schools, spit and polish, being in uniform, making muster, and other contrived displays of propriety regularly intrude to offset complete informality (Orwell, 1953). In these organizations, as in the military, there seems to be an almost explicit awareness of how these ritualized observances are necessary to keep their members "up to snuff." Social awareness of this principle comes out clearly in the classic tale of the new ship's captain who has succeeded someone who has "let things go" and must now run an excessively "tight ship" (Cobb, 1935; Heggen, 1946). The new captain must do battle with an overdeveloped and subversive collusion of friends. In at least the movie version of this tale, "old hardnose" is heartily hated until the first battle proves the value of discipline and shoe polish. Then "old hardnose" is begrudgingly loved and respected almost as much as John Wayne.

An example very different from the military is the mental hospital. The inmates of these hospitals do not march, parade inspections, or salute their keepers. Because mental patients have chronically violated some of the rules of public propriety, they are usually thought to be incapable of observing any of these rules. The resultant social order is a peculiar mixture of tolerance and tyranny (Goffman, 1961a, pp. 125–169). Mental patients are allowed to pick their noses, leave their trousers unbuttoned, and use obscenities. At the same time, the mental patient is often manipulated almost as a "thing" by being put to bed, kept doped on tranquilizers, and physically restrained where it is thought necessary.[5]

For the mental patient this social order seems to divest him of either a real or a socially proper self. Since there are no evident rules of public propriety, the patient seems to have no benchmark against which he can bring into relief his own willfull departures from "mere compliance."[6] But since there is also no socially proper role for the mental patient, he is equally unable to present himself as someone capable of self constraint and a contrived performance. In the mental hospital, the net result seems to be a very rudimentary social order where neither formal nor informal social relations are elaborated much beyond the isolated individual or dyad. Thus, unlike prisons, mental hospitals seem to lack an intricate and subversive informal order for either "beating the system" or preserving the peace among the inmates themselves (Szasz, 1963). Oddly, this does not mean that mental hospitals are the scene of constant violence or a "war of all against all." Perhaps Hobbes was wrong after all; the absence of a social order to regulate human conduct may not result in vicious exploitation but mere apathy and withdrawal from social contacts altogether.

Certainly friendships are made in those situations where ecological, technological, and chronological conditions do not allow people to keep separate front and back regions. Yet, in a way, these are friendships made under duress and to some extent people may recognize in them a note of coercion or necessity. Like commercially contrived "get togethers" they lack the surest signs of voluntarism and spontaneity. As a result, friendships begun un-

5. Some of which is documented in the film, *Titticut Follies.*
6. Although Kesey (1962) gives his central character a heightened individuality by playing on this very theme. But it seems safe to say that such heightened individuality occurs mainly in novels about mental hospitals and very seldom in real mental hosiptals. It should be added that these effects of mental hospitals have not gone unnoticed by their staffs, and the recent move toward more "outpatient" treatment is in part a response to this situation.

der these confined circumstances seem to have a rather short half
life once they are removed to more spacious quarters. Despite
their own protests to the contrary, army buddies seldom see each
other after they are discharged (Little, 1964). Cell mates in
prison ("cellies") make a concerted effort to avoid one another on
release despite the general absence of alternative associations
(Glaser, 1964, pp. 362–401). Ex-mental patients seem to avoid
one another like the plague (Landy and Singer, 1961), and the
chorus girl who has married well may have only a polit word for
those she greeted in a more ribald manner. It is easy to dismiss
such past friendships because they do not rest on the sure coin
of spontaneity, which is assumed necessary to a completed
friendship.

DEVIATION AS THE BASIS FOR FRIENDSHIP

If friendship is not a prescribed or socially determined relationship, it is still a patterned and orderly institution. The very basic
assumption friends must make about one another is that each is
going beyond a mere presentation of self in compliance with
"social dictates."[7] Inevitably, this makes friendship a somewhat
deviant relationship because the surest test of personal disclosure
is a violation of the rules of public propriety. This, however, does
not mean that friends are simply disorderly or ribald companions.
Friendship demands a systematic violation of public morality
and it can be as compelling and restrictive a relationship as any
other.

The logic of friendship is a simple transformation of the rules
of public propriety into their opposite. Friends can touch each
other where strangers cannot. Friends can swear or become exceptionally pious around one another. Friends can entertain
subversive or utopian political ideologies that would be laughed
at in public circumstances. If, tomorrow, it became publicly
proper for strangers to spit upon meeting one another, friends
would probably assume that they have the right to neglect this
duty.

7. A point that seems glossed over in Goffman (1959), although not in
his *Stigma* (1963).

Friends cannot, then, behave arbitrarily around one another. First, the rules of public propriety represent the touchstone from which friends must start and the diverse paths they must follow. Friendships may diverge from either side of public propriety, tending, for instance, toward an extreme of prudery or an extreme of license. Within these two options, there are numerous other branches along which friendships can be elaborated. Generally these elaborations of friendship follow institutional sectors already dividing the application of the rules of propriety. Drinking partners, for example, have to stay pretty much within that sector of life that emphasizes consumptory practices to the exclusion of, say, work or practical politics. Similarly, friends who have challenged the rules of propriety surrounding sexual relations cannot easily go on to be equally irreverent toward institutions or establishments (e.g., planned parenthood, cocktail lounges, coeducation) that somewhat liberalize sexual relations. Violations of the rules of public propriety in any one institutional sector seem tacitly to exclude similar violations in at least some other institutional sectors. No doubt the line between these institutional sectors is often fuzzy, and they are not always mutually exclusive. Nonetheless, there is a tenuous opposition between most institutions because they must compete for common resources and loyalties. The family competes with the peer group, work with recreation, and political involvement with scholarly detachment. If a person makes fun of the Republican party, he will be thought a Democrat. If he makes fun of both parties, he will be thought a radical or socialist. The institutional sectors of society consist of many competing camps and by leaving one of them, an individual is thrust, willingly or unwillingly, into another.[8]

Second, once friendships have been formed they are guided by a series of precedents especially compelling because they are regarded as the heartfelt symptoms of one's real self. "Going back" on a friend or disclaiming previous self-disclosures are especially damaging because they expose one as a "hypocrite" or opportunist. Indeed, friendship can be a very confining relationship

8. In fact, an utter rejection of all organized life thrusts a person into an acknowledged camp: e.g., "Oh so you don't believe in anything. Anarchist!"

precisely because it is based on voluntary deviations from the rules of propriety.

Thus, while friendship always involves some degree of deviation, it is also a way of stabilizing relationships and of narrowing down the options among which people may select. As an institution, then, friendship helps society gravitate toward a more determinate order, although this order is not necessarily the same as that described by idealized values or codified rules and laws. Yet it is order itself that is fundamental to society; slight or even major deviations from the ideal values of a society may be harmless so long as people can still find an orderly world within which to negotiate their way. Where one must choose between them, having an orderly social world may be an improvement over one that is morally correct.

In any event, friendships develop from and subsist on personal deviations that are especially minor and inconsequential. Behavior in compliance with the rules of public propriety consists of suggestive actions. It is a way of "giving one's word" that he will ignore or not bring up embarrassing social differences or universal failings. In turn, failures to comply only with the rules of propriety are also only suggestive rather than terminal actions. By swearing or being too pious, a person indicates that he will not gracefully steer away from "sensitive" issues or half-hidden human vices. Such a posture may hurt people's feelings and embarrass others. But violating only the rules of propriety goes no further than this. Properly forewarned, people can now segregate themselves before the battle lines form or outright predation starts. Indeed, as most professional criminals know, a strict compliance with the rules of public propriety is one way of beguiling the victim until he has exhausted his opportunities to retreat.[9] The individual who is gauche or obscene at the start warns his potential victims while there is still time to get away.

The rules of propriety, then, serve as a sort of pedestrian early warning system, allowing people to retreat before actual conflict takes place. They are the type of rules we like to have around so that they can be broken; for it is by the breakage of the rules of propriety that we are warned of real dangers. Perhaps this is why

9. A point illustrated in David W. Maurer's *The Big Con* (1962).

many people simply dismiss the rules of public propriety as sheer ritual or an exercise in social constraint that has no apparent objective. But even such complaints as these show how the rules of public propriety can be used to notify others of one's own individuality.

Where individuals violate the rules of public propriety and find themselves in uncritical hands, the first steps toward friendship have already been made. Like partners in crime, individuals find themselves bound together in a private morality where the chief guidelines are their own expressed sentiments. Friends have a natural interest in preserving this private morality, not only because it is easy to live with, but because its reality seems so irrefutable and reliable. There are, of course, baser interests that make friendship a self-governing and persistent relation. Friends know "too much" about one another to chance easily their alienation from each other and a sort of mutual blackmail may force their relation forward despite a lack of gratification on the part of one member. The net result is that friendships simply tend to persist so long as they are at all convenient and not shown to be "false."

It is obvious, of course, that not all disclosures of self are attended by the good fortune of friendship. At the outset, persons who depart from public propriety always risk being rebuffed and left standing without companions. Indeed, it is because of these risks that the early stages of friendships are often filled with a certain excitement and pleasure. As people move away from the safe course of public propriety, their apprehensions grow and the benefits of finding oneself in uncritical hands are magnified by the relief experienced from uncertainty and possible rejection. In the early stages of friendship, then, there is a "honeymoon" period very much like what couples are supposed to experience shortly after marriage; each new step toward self-disclosure is doubly rewarding because it relieves one's apprehensions as well as flattering one's self. Afterwards, when mutual acceptance is more or less guaranteed, some of the pleasure and excitement of friendship and marriage are gone.

But the risks undertaken in the service of friendship are real and often they result in embarrassment, hurt feelings, and subsequent avoidance. Willfully or not, individuals have strayed away from the safe course of public propriety and drawn a bad lot. Ordinarily this sort of misstep is attributed to a "clash of personalities," which is commonly the case. People are not all alike and the information they may divulge about themselves is apt to create even more variation. In any society the chances are substantial that you will run up against someone who "cannot stand you." That is what makes friendship a very special relationship.

Self Exposure and Institutional Restrictions on Friendship

GUARDED EXPOSURES OF SELF

Beyond the personal information about themselves that individuals cannot safely share, there are several structural barriers to friendship. The most obvious of these are status differences that fall into a hierarchical mold. Across status barriers, invitations to friendship arouse suspicions because they may denote either a conflict of interests or ulterior motives. Improper overtures from persons of a higher status are often taken as disguised attempts to "take advantage" of underlings who will have little power to retaliate on subsequent occasions. Lower-status individuals who solicit the personal attention of their superiors are suspect of being "brown nosers" or of seeking favors. In either case, friendship between persons at different levels in the *same hierarchy* are thought to compromise one's judgment because it balances a person's duties against his personal inclinations. The very fact of status differences, then, undermines the basis of friendship, which is the assumption that individuals are acting of their own will rather than out of calculation or connivance. This, of course, does not mean that persons of markedly different social status never become friends: only that they probably will have trouble once they are friends.

Ordinarily, then, status differences foreclose the issue of friendship, because they deter people from violating the rules of propriety in the first place. This, however, is not invariably the case because a number of status relations have the explicit purpose of inquiring into the private character of one member. Doctors, lawyers, priests, and psychiatrists, for example, have both the right and duty to ask questions and make observations that exceed the usual limits of public propriety. Thus, in the case of these roles, status differences alone are not a sufficient barrier to friendship (or exploitation and favoritism) and additional barriers must be constructed.

The most substantial of these barriers is probably the asymmetry in the amounts of personal information each party to the relationship makes available to the other. Take, for example, the doctor-patient relation. Doctors can cloak themselves in white robes; patients must disrobe at request. Doctors can ask about one's social diseases, sex practices, or drinking habits. Doctors themselves may mutter only a few words in liturgical Latin, nod sagely, consult occult charts, and end the session with a coded prescription meant to inform a druggist rather than the patient. Doctors can thump on one's body and examine one's privy parts; it would be thought very odd if the patient attempted to do the same thing even to his own body. The doctor is properly addressed by his title while the patient may be referred to either by his first name or as "Mr." or "Mrs."

This asymmetry in information control is paralleled in the relations of lawyer–client, priest–layman and psychiatrist–patient. The use of cloaks or disguising uniforms is common, although less so among psychiatrists and lawyers than among priests or ministers. Proper titles are uniformly present although lawyers in the United States have been unsuccessful in getting their title ("counselor") used outside the courtroom itself. In all these status relations is a technical and occult language drawing heavily from the deader portions of Greek and Latin. Touching another person's body is more variable; generally only doctors and ministers can get away with it. For the senior member of the relationship, however, there are always unreciprocated rights to inquire into the more sordid and improper aspects of one's past. Lawyers can question and examine their own clients and cross-examine the clients of another lawyer. Some clergymen can require regular confessions while other clergymen stand ready to hear confessions.

Among all these status relations, the psychiatrist or psychologist has the most unusual extraordinary access to what a person might call his "real self." In at least some psychiatric circles, psychiatrists must go beyond the limits of propriety that the patient himself can manage to recount or remember. In order to construct for the patient a self so discrepant with public propriety that its reality is undeniable or irrefutable, the patient must show "resistance" or signs of denial or outrage. It is exactly at this point, however, that some psychiatrists feel that they reach the bedrock of one's self and existence. This seems to carry to rather extreme limits the general principle that what is most improper in a person's thoughts and deeds is also most diagnostic of his real self.

Since this asymmetry in information exchange is so great, there is little danger of friendship and along with it neither favoritism nor brown nosing will often cross these status differences. Instead, the difficulty of managing such relations shifts dramatically to center on the problem of avoiding self-mortification for the junior member. (Goffman, 1961, 1–124). Where people mutually disclose themselves as something less than the ultimate of public propriety, friendship provides a safe harbor where judgements of worth shift to fit performance. At a minimum, people who have mutually disclosed themselves can simply run and avoid one another. With doctors, lawyers, ministers, and psychiatrists, however, neither friendship nor avoidance is a convenient and inexpensive alternative. For the lower-status client, patient, or layman, self-mortification is a very real threat and requires exceptional social arrangements.

The first of these social arrangements is the prestige or honor bestowed on clergymen, doctors, psychiatrists, and lawyers. People in these positions are expected to keep in confidence one's failings, not to smirk when they see you nor to be nonplussed when told about your most outrageous thoughts and deeds. A great deal of care goes into the selection and training of those people who must be a party to our darker moments. Because of this investment into their selection and training, we are apt to think that lawyers, clergymen, psychiatrists, and doctors are trustworthy men who will not spread tales about our misshapened bodies or irregular pasts. Nonetheless, we also insist upon bribing them by a high income, which makes it unnecessary for these honored men to look for opportunities outside their regular income. There is, then, a large element of sacredness or legitimacy that must be attributed to doctors, clergymen, and psychiatrists. We educate and pay them well not only to keep them honest but to assure ourselves that they are as honorable a group of men as we hope they are.

What are often referred to as the "free professions" are a second set of social arrangements that preserve us from self-mortification in these asymmetric exchanges of information. Doctors, priests, lawyers, and psychiatrists enjoy uncommon freedom from either the temptation or the necessity to divulge the dirty details they know about other people. Ordinarily, doctors, lawyers, psychiatrists, and clergymen work in isolated establishments where there is no one looking over their shoulder and no immediate obligation to report on what they have just discovered from their clients. It is easy for them to keep their silence simply because of spatial and bureaucratic arrangements. Only at rare intervals must they report in to say what they have heard or done. Also, these free professionals remain almost unchallenged in the veracity of what they have to say about someone else's character. They may refuse to comment on their clients, although priests and lawyers are more privileged in what they must communicate than psychiatrists and doctors. Special vows of poverty, chastity, and public service especially protect the priest from the allegation that he is in league with his clients (Coser, 1964, 880–885). Above all, priests, lawyers, and psychiatrists are considered experts whose judgments can be questioned by only a small group of people or no one.

It is not by accident, I suspect, that these free professionals minister to what are the recognizable portions of a person's total identity in Western society at least. The body, legal citizenship, mind, and soul include most of what we cherish about ourselves and dearly hope to place in safe hands. We are only being responsible—at least cautious—when we place these bits and pieces of ourselves in the hands of someone who can say about us pretty much what we tell him to say.

Of course not all clergymen, lawyers, doctors, or psychiatrists are equally trusted or equally honored. The doctor is especially respected because his certification is bestowed by an impartial institution and grounded in an unchallenged technical knowhow.

Lawyers are screened and certified in the same way, but they can only partially protect us from self-mortification. Court judges play a larger role here, and accordingly they encroach very much upon the lawyer's authority and prestige. The psychiatrist has the same type of credential as the doctor or lawyer, but his judgment of patients is still secondary to a lawyer's or court judge's. Ministers and priests may be self-selected or accredited by institutions that are partial to signs of faithfulness and actual performance. They may or may not be honored men who can or will preserve laymen from self-mortification.

Within the courtroom itself, this little status hierarchy of the free professions is brought into high relief. The coroner presents his testimony without challenge because no one else in the court is thought able to challenge him. The defending lawyer presents his case but he can be challenged by the prosecuting attorney, and especially by the judge. A testifying psychologist can give an "opinion" on someone's sanity but he can be challenged by practically everyone in court except the jury (Simon, 1967). A priest or minister can serve as a "character witness" or at worst keep their silence; in any case their testimony is subject to challenge from every quarter. Thus, if one wants to avoid all possibility of self-mortification it is best to select confessors whose testimony is least challengeable. On the whole, we have done rather well to get our doctors, lawyers, psychologists, and ministers into the upper two deciles of our prestige ranking system so that at least most people will believe what these experts say (or do not say) about us (Hodge, Siegel and Rossi, 1964, 286–302).

UNGUARDED EXPOSURES OF SELF

We make friends by exposing ourselves, and friendship is a way of saving ourselves from self-mortification once we have exposed our "real selves." The rules surrounding the free professions are an additional safeguard against self-mortification where self-exposure is unavoidable. Friendship and the free professions, however, are only a partial refuge from the hazards of self-exposure and self-mortification. Well beyond these relatively safe options are others where a person's private life and unredeeming improprieties must be made public and bandied about among all those who care to listen. Many people, particularly those of low income or status, cannot secure a free professional to protect them and friendship is sometimes forbidden by either personality clashes or status differences.

There are, then, several relationships where information exchanges are asymmetrical but unrelieved by either the possibilities of friendship or "professional treatment." The public assistance case worker, for instance, must usually violate the secrets of his client in order to serve a public agency. Policemen are hired explicitly for the purpose of leveling charges against people and helping to prove that their conduct is at best improper. Obviously public assistance workers and policemen may subvert their duties by sheltering persons from the full light of public exposure. Spys, informers, and secret agents have a clearer and dirtier social charge. But these impostors feed off society at its uninstitutionalized margins rather than help compose a portion of its regular scenario or complement of characters. Policemen, public assistance workers, prison guards, and probation workers are publicly announced informers purposefully planted among us to divulge our shortcomings and improprieties.

For both the alters and incumbents of these roles, there is no easy solution to the asymmetric disclosures of information required of them. Some exposure of impropriety is bound to occur. If the senior member to the relationship relents and "overlooks" improprieties, then he is "compromised" or loses status. He becomes the corrupted cop, the public assistance worker who goes into collusion with his client, or the prison screw who is "too easy." Conversely, a strict observance of the formal rules or their roles makes the public assistance worker, the policeman, and prison guard appear tyrants bent on the mortification of their alters.

So far analysts have thought mainly in terms of the self-mortification of the lower-ranking member to these status relations. But the same relationship may be almost as damaging to its senior partner. The policeman, public assistance worker, or prison guard cannot be trusting people, like the free professionals, who exhibit in their everyday behavior the noblest ideals and most sensitive feelings of Western civilization. They must be hard, cautious, and quick to find fault. We cannot afford to hold such people up too high in our status hierarchy, for then they would be able to bring to bear upon us all so harsh and unremitting a set of standards that everyone would fail. Certainly their authority ought not be such that they can challenge the judgment of those who stand in the upper half of our status hierarchy; accordingly we find that at least policemen and welfare workers fall just about at dead center in our occupational rankings (Hodge, Siegel and Rossi, 1964, 286–302). This may not be an entirely fair way of protecting the higher-status members of our society, but it is adequate.

Unfair or not, such a social arrangement compromises those occupations that must mortify their counterparts or eschew friendship as a sort of "corruption." Since they cannot be trusting, generous, forgiving, or unchallenged experts, policemen, prison guards, and other "custodians" suffer a degree of status degradation that parallels the degrees of mortification they must impose on their junior counterparts. Such custodians cannot give voice to the finer social graces or our emblems of honor and respect; unchallenged expertise, good will, and sensitivity. By treating their clients badly, these custodial personnel are dragged down in the same mire. If some people are to be treated like swine, then their caretakers will be treated like swineherds. Admittedly this analogy is overdrawn, but it brings into relief the inexorable logic that makes each of us both victims and victimizers.

Certainly asymmetric information exchanges unsecured by the guarantees of the free professions do not rule out the possibilities of friendship. Policemen, prison guards, and probation workers do become friends with the people they are supposed to arraign before higher courts of law (Ohlin, Piven, and Pappenfort, 1956, 211–225). But such personal choices threaten further the status of those occupations unable to speak alone for their clients; friendship between subordinate and superordinate suggests corruption and threatens the status of both parties. Friendship is possible, but it is a high risk venture.

The Private Culture of Friendship

THE STAGING OF FRIENDSHIP

We know a great deal more about friendship choices than we know about friendship itself. Friendship is supposed to be a warm, lasting, and very secure relationship. Our data on friendship, however, skirt around the edges of the institution and look at it only from the outside. We know very little about the internal ferment, longevity, and special morality of friendship. Friends do not simply "live happily ever after" and certainly there is more to it than its primary and terminal junctures.

Even these primary and terminal junctures of friendship are insufficiently characterized in the literature. First, the events and situations that lead to friendship have not been carefully matched with the meanings friends impose on these events and situations. The terms "mutual access" or "social distance," for example, do not adequately convey the inferences, innuendos, and subtleties people draw from them. Two ladies who meet in the laundromat are not just near one another; they may be badly dressed, poorly groomed, and in general ill prepared to lay claim to the rules of public propriety. Low social distance, on the other hand, may simply mean that people are shoved into such close confines that they cannot avoid touching one another or making evident other signs that are taken as an invitation to additional personal improprieties. Sheer frequency of contact, for instance, may be interpreted as a purposeful solicitation to intimacy. We need two different languages, one to describe the objective circumstances for the onset of friendship and another to describe the meanings people read into these circumstances. And it is important that we not allow either of these languages to crowd out the other because both are necessary to identify cultural differences.

Second, we know very little about the incidence of those situations that permit or require different populations to go beyond a presentation of self that is only ordinary or very proper. It is frequently observed that middle-income people have more voluntaristic affiliations than do lower-income people (Tomeh, 1962, 85–102). This may reflect a difference in interpersonal skills, in aggregate personal tendencies, or only the cumulative effects of numerous minor, almost trivial, situational differences that allow middle-class people to make a sharp contrast between proper and improper presentations of self. Middle-class people generally live in independent dwelling units, which allow for a good deal of privacy, a graduated approach toward intimacy, and a wide range of personal possessions to signal one's real self. Middle-income people often take part in public rituals and ceremonies and can draw a very sharp line between what they really are and what they are expected to be. Movie stars and public performers are so subject to constant surveillance that their real selves stand out in such broad relief that they must have "fan clubs" to meet the supply of eager friends. These are clandestine and fragmentary observations, which show only how little we know about the incidence of situations that provoke friendship. It is not that we are uninformed about how social distance relates to friendship; but that we do not know how social distance is distributed in various populations.

Third, the inner world of friendship is not an untroubled and even experience. At the outset, I have suggested, friends experience a sort of "honeymoon" period where the pleasant experience of acceptance is amplified by a relief from contrary apprehensions. Friendships subsist on little stories about past exploits that defied public propriety; but after a while these stories may grow stale and there will be a need for new material. This new material may be supplied by joint demonstrations of impropriety where friends manage to offend outsiders to their mutual satisfaction. Friends cling together in a sort of subterranean plot against the explicit rulings of the wider society. Undoubtedly this makes friendship a sort of uneasy balancing between personal and social obligations. Friendship must be constantly renewed and negotiated simply because it cannot be assumed on the basis of prescriptive social rulings. This is not an attempt to indicate the stages or phases of friendship, but to show how fully speculation must fill in for an absence of close observation.

Fourth, friendships "break up" as do marital partners and lovers. Often friends just move to different parts of the country or find some other excuse for neglecting one another. But there are also friends who become enemies before they stop being friends. Aside from sheer separation, we know little about what are the events and their meaning which draw friends apart. This is an area where the subtleties of our culture may be unmasked and analyzed. So far, however, we have no study of friendship separation comparable to our many studies of marital separation.

On the whole, then, we know little about the content of friendship except that it occurs among people who are "relatively
similar." In between its beginning and end there is a story that
badly needs to be told. Friendship presents one of the little
dramas of everyday life, and by understanding it we may be able
to tease out some of the generic patterns of social life where
prescriptive norms do not tell the full story.

THE SELF IN FRIENDSHIP

Ordinarily individuals think of their real selves as being contained
inside their skins and, perhaps, most concentrated near their
hearts, brains, or genitals. It is only after reflection and some
argument that an individual might agree that portions of his real
self are differentially concentrated in a series of concentric circles
reaching out beyond his skin and clothing. In fact, what often
makes friendship easy is the low risk with which an individual
can plant emblems of himself in some of the outer and most public
circles around his body.

Most distant from an individual's body is his selection of material possessions; his books, automobile, furniture, paintings, and
the like. These items are rather like "trial balloons," which can be
used to alert other people about one's real self without drawing
them into possible disagreements. Others can simply assess one's
possessions and then quietly go away if they find them to their
disliking. Alternatively, if one wants to, he can make much of
someone else's possessions and how they represent in some singu-
lar fashion a shared taste that departs from mere conventionality.
For this reason, individuals often select personal possessions that
are distinctive, offbeat, or shocking. Teenagers embellish their
automobiles with foxtails and decals. Bachelors display on their
walls an outrageous nude or leave around a well-thumbed copy
of *Playboy*. Society matrons may strategically place in public
view a copy of *Ramparts* or a calendar with a Nordic Christ.

Here again the general principle seems to be that one's possessions must overreach the safe limits of public propriety by suggesting either an excess of virtue or vice. But this outermost circle
of self representation is a rather low risk investment in the poten-
tials of friendship, because it permits people gradually to disclose

their real selves rather than force a full exposure of self at the outset.

This gradation of self-disclosure is especially well represented in the rooms of a home. Being able to approach a home from the rear and to converse in the kitchen will usually provide individuals with the feeling that they can be surer of each other's real selves than if they were constrained to meet first in the living room. Sharing a bedroom may require a further level of intimacy at one's next meeting. Sleeping in the same bed goes even further in the same direction and perhaps the furthest one can go in the same household is in sharing a bathroom. Step by step, then, the rooms of a house invite or forbid additional stages of intimacy and self disclosure.

This gradient of intimacy, however, steepens as it gets closer to the individual's skin and privy parts. A person's clothing, for example, is something that always travels along with him. It cannot be easily hidden and, except in the case of uniforms, is judged an item of personal choice. Ordinary courtesy also requires that we comment upon new clothing or exceptional clothing. In turn, comments on one's clothing are taken very personally whereas most of one's other possessions can be represented as a joint or familial purchase. Observations on a person's clothing, then, draw very close to the person himself and jar open the doors to further self-disclosure or shut these doors altogether (Stone, 1962, 86–118).

A person's body is the last and most sensitive perimeter in this gradation of self-disclosure. Once you are able to touch a person, even a failure to respond can be an invitation to further intimacy. Also, at each step along the way, the areas of one's body that can be touched signal the present stage of the relationship as well as the forthcoming moves that can be made. Among those who can touch us, some have got only so far as a handshake while others have advanced to putting their hand on our waists or shoulder. Adolescents in a streetcorner gang have usually advanced to the point where they can "gouch" each other in the rear. Athletes typically have the right to slap each other on the rear. Lovers, in their turn, may go still further. In general, as one moves closer to a person past his personal possessions or the living room, and starts trespassing upon his body, it becomes less and less possible to remain unresponsive and mute. At some point it becomes necessary to cut short these token moves or encourage them along.

In no area is this sort of cautious and self-governing progression more evident than in dating patterns among middle-class Americans. Boy-girl relations start in the most proper manner, often with a "blind date" where neither partner even knows who the other is. From that point on, each progressive move either cuts short the relationship altogether or lays the groundwork for the next move. On their first date, couples are either badly disappointed or they at least hold hands and make light conversation. Kissing is a problem.[10] Authorities suggest it should not be done on the first date but that makes a kiss all the more significant if it is freely given and badly desired. From this point on, unmarried couples can progress to petting, "deep petting," and the trauma of whether or not they will have intercourse.

At each step along the way, dating partners either cut short their relationship altogether or grant liberties that serve as promissory notes, which can be cashed in to require even greater liberties at their next meeting (Waller, 1937, 727–34). Kissing on one's second date means that one can pet on the next date. Petting on the third date means that one might try a french kiss on the fourth date.[11] From thereon the regions on one's body that can be explored or shared are especially difficult to decide without also deciding upon such questions as marriage or temporary cohabitation.

As the stages of dating advance they also become more determinative of the next stage. Not much is lost by never asking out a blind date for a second time. Kissing on the first date, however, is a promissory note to do more on the next date. Eventually, the blunt fact of premarital pregnancy may foreclose all choices in the matter and make marriage a foregone issue. This progressive closure upon a single and permanent social relationship among individuals seems to be a general pattern among friends as well as

10. For a recommended staging of dating relations see Ann Landers' booklet, *Datings Do's and Don'ts.*

11. For a markedly different series of such stages see *Ching Pei Mei* (*The Gold Lotus,* 1960).

dating partners. It evolves rather directly from the concentric rings that surround an individual and always make him vulnerable to a passive or active review by other people. A person can never really fully hide himself, for even a total neglect of one's private possessions, home, clothing, and body will invite at least some attention and interpretation. One's values and impulses, then, cannot simply remain unknown because they lie outside the skin. Nonetheless, invitations to friendship are easily refused so long as they gather only about one's outermost perimeter. Beyond that point friendship becomes more nearly a foregone conclusion as individuals take steps that cannot be easily retracted. Inevitably then, one finds friends, marital partners, and lovers who are regretful of having advanced so far that they have reached "the point of no return."[12]

Conclusion

Friendship is a very generalized form of affiliation, which in principle can reach across every barrier of social organization. Because it can extend so far and in so many directions, friendship is an especially important interstitial institution that can link individuals who are unrelated by prescriptive institutons. More than this, friendship is also a way of "going around" social conventions that get in the way of substantive social responsibilities and aims. Herein lies one of the great advantages of friendship; for no society seems able to work fully according to its formal norms. There must be some room for deviation, and friendship allows people to draw off in a private morality within which they can make the adjustments and rearrangements required to "get something done."

Friendship is supposed to be a warm and secure relationship and a goal in its own right. What gives friendship its most desired features, however, is its ability to assure people of their mutual reality, dependability, or sincerity. This seems a rather simple "reward" compared to money, food, or sex. But this betrays about us what seems a very elementary search for a social order removed

12. A theme well developed in the novel by John P. Marquand, *Point of No Return* (1952).

from obvious conventions and founded on a sort of bedrock of seeming reality. Apparently the fragility of conventional social life is so obvious that we are gratified simply by knowing what someone is "really like."

In fact, as I have suggested, friends may especially like one another because they are somewhat unconventional or improper. This casts upon our notion of norms and values a somewhat different perspective than that common among sociologists. Often norms and values are described as if they dictate or determine in a rather mechanical fashion the behavior of people. But in friendship the norms of propriety are primarily a benchmark against which people can be judged and partialed out according to what they are really like. Norms and values, in this instance, help give meaning to what people do, but these cultural rulings do not directly determine what people do.

No doubt this general principle carries over into many areas of social life; people use social norms and values, they do not simply obey these norms and values. They use these norms and values to read into someone's behavior some meaning and to forecast his next piece of behavior. As a result it is possible for us to see people as "far out," "stodgy," "dull," or "easygoing." These forms of behavior may or may not be sanctionable. They may excite agreement, they may be reprehensible, or they may be a matter of indifference. In highly differentiated societies a single set of modal rulings simply cannot capture all or even most of the forms of behavior required. Some more flexible basis for mutual personal evaluation is needed if people are to cooperate rather than just do "what's right." In most modern and highly differentiated societies the "norms" may function as only a sort of reference point against which various groups can define themselves and their fellow members. As with the mean on an IQ test, practically no one scores at exactly this level but certainly the notion of an average or "normal IQ" helps us separate ourselves into groupings like "dullards," "highbrows," "brains," "stupes," "morons," "geniuses," "eggheads," and "ordinary folk."

In many modern and complex societies, then, norms and values may function primarily as a reference point for measuring departures from conventional behavior and forecasting additional departures. Matza has persuasively argued this point, saying that social norms are primarily a way of helping people to predict rather than to determine each others' behavior (Matza, 1964). I do not want to enlarge upon his statement but instead to emphasize the way social values and norms continue to help give meaning to a person's behavior no matter how deviant he is. The person who acts "too hastily," or "talks too much" can still be defined by a common system of normative coordinates. We may dislike such a person or want to join him. It is, however, our common normative system that allows us to make this judgment.

In the case of friendship we are enabled to define people according to how they hold to or depart from the norms of public propriety. We may diverge first from either side of the rules of public propriety, becoming "too proper" or "too improper." From there on we may elaborate our path out according to a tree of contrastive institutional sectors. If we make fun of liberals we are assumed to be conservatives. If we openly make light of the American family, we are taken for Communists or rogue males. Each move we make away from one institutional section implies commitment to its alternative. This sort of contrastive structure, which branches out from the golden mean and forms a tree of pluralism, seems to be a very generic process to all social behavior. These contrastive structures are present in our language, reaching into even its phonology. And as Levi-Strauss has argued, a system of binary contrasts that bifurcate about the "mean" may be the most universal characteristic of all human cultures (Levi-Strauss, 1966).

What may be most remarkable about friendship as an institution, however, is how nearly it constitutes a self-governing system that comes into existence as it is needed while its constituent elements all operate to the same end. In a modern and highly differentiated society, a vast number of people find the rules of public propriety different from their own feelings and inclinations. By departing from these rules of public propriety, however, people are able to secure themselves in the eyes of other people who are also looking a bit beyond the conventional. Once self-exposure occurs, it becomes progressively fateful and ties individuals to the precedents they have made. Friendship is like a fishhook; the further it goes in the harder it is to pull out.

Yet friendship does not mean an utter departure from social life, its values or its norms. Friendship is above all a private relationship in which the members must exclude other people or offend them by bold displays of comaraderie. If friends invite all others into their private morality, then they lose the very special covenant they have authored. Friendship may be deviant, but it is seldom a plot into which large masses of people can be joined.

Friendship, then, is a benign institution, for while it segregates defectors from the normative rulings of society it gives their subterranean world little chance to grow. It provides alternative ways for doing things when the formal structure of society is clearly inadequate. And it gives the individual a very strong sense of his own and other peoples' reality when the normative rules of society have come to appear especially artificial and fragile.

Friendships and
Friendly Relations

In this essay the author views the personal and societal functions of friendship as less than uniformly positive and shared importantly with a less intimate social relationship, the friendly relation. The characteristics of these two types are distinguished, and the initiation, development, and change of each are described. The character of interaction within friendships and friendly relations is expounded, with special reference to ambivalence, conflict, and the role of third parties.

This paper focuses on distinguishing *friendship,* an intimate interpersonal relationship involving each individual as a personal entity, from a *friendly relation,* an outgrowth of a formal role relationship and a preliminary stage in the development of a friendship. I explore the differences between them, and the formation and maintenance of each, while I consider why friendly relations are prevalent in our society today.

It has been argued that ideally men seek to establish enduring relationships with others, built upon the total person and absolute psychological intimacy. Friendship and marriage are two forms of interpersonal relationship that at times in various societies have been conceived of in this way. Despite our frequent emphasis upon these enduring, intimate relationships, it is difficult for these ideal relationships to occur.[1] Since friendships require a high level of psychological intimacy, they involve a great deal of ourselves. Simmel noted years ago that "such complete intimacy becomes probably more and more difficult as differentiation among men increases. Modern man possibly has too much to hide to sustain a friendship in the ancient sense" (1950, p. 326). Although friendship relationships in which there is considerable intimacy and considerable involvement of self might be difficult to achieve, men seem to search for them. But they frequently satisfy themselves with another type of relationship, a friendly relation.

This paper will indicate that the friendly relation that involves limited aspects of individuals is a relationship that can be distinguished from friendship, and that in many cases we prefer to form friendly relations rather than friendships.

Desirability of Friendly Relations

In a complex society such as ours, we are involved in relationships with many people. Many are prescribed role relationships. We form friendly relations with many people in such role relationships. A friendly relation may facilitate the interaction associated with fulfilling formal role requirements. For example, when we establish friendly relations with fellow workers whose cooperation we rely upon, we feel that they will do what is formally expected of them and more, for often if they adhere strictly to their formal role, our work will be more difficult than necessary.[2]

1. The emphasis on such relationships and the difficulties involved in attaining and maintaining them is referred to in Simmel (1950, pp. 122–32, 324–29, 379–95); Waller (1938, Parts I and II); and McCall and Simmons (1966, Chaps. 6 and 7).

2. In addition to facilitating our performances of formal roles, friendly relations perhaps serve as insurance policies for us. This "friendly" basis of interaction can protect us because it results in a "safe" degree of closeness to others. Lofland (1969, p. 8) has noted that strangers and intimates are most likely to do us personal harm and that establishing an "acquaintanceship" is perhaps the safest thing to do in terms of personal injury.

Also, friendly relations are desirable *because* they lack many characteristics of friendships while still providing us with a pleasant basis of association. We are frequently ambivalent about intimate relationships such as friendships, for we encounter in them considerable costs as well as considerable rewards. One can sustain friendly relations with several others at one time, but many friendships are difficult to maintain because considerable expenditures are involved in each. Since we are involved in many role relationships with others, it is generally more profitable to establish friendly relations with a number of those people than friendships with a few of them.

A friendly relation can develop into a friendship; however, it usually does not because we do not wish to establish friendships with many individuals and because of the burden of our preexisting commitments. The commitments we have shape the time and energy we feel we have available to spend with someone new; they tend to keep us from becoming involved in new relationships that require extensive commitments. Most of the time we are not actively seeking to form friendships. We develop friendships when we have found a friendly relation with another rewarding and want to secure those rewards enough to rearrange our commitments.

Friendly Relations in Contrast with Friendships

The positions that we occupy in the social structure and the roles we play shape the formal role relationships we engage in with others, "but the demands of formal positions do not account for the distribution of the more sociable, relatively voluntary, and unprescribed aspects of a person's interactions or for his violations and abrogations of those demands." (McCall and Simmons, 1966, p. 232). Since friendly relations and friendships both involve individuals beyond the demands of any formal role relationship they might have and a friendly relation can develop into a friendship, we must clarify what distinguishes each.

VOLUNTARY INTERACTION

Friendly relations and friendships require voluntary interaction. In friendly relations, however, such interaction is more limited than it is in friendships. Studies have found that people tend to interact most frequently, at least at first, with individuals in physical proximity (Festinger *et al*, 1959, pp. 33–59; Gullahorn, 1952; Homans, 1954). Generally, sociologists are talking about friendly relations rather than friendships when they consider proximity based interaction in dormitories, offices, and among neighbors. People thrown together in these situations frequently engage in interaction beyond what is required by formal roles. If voluntary interaction is limited to the times and settings provided by formal role relationships, as it often is, a friendly relation but not a friendship exists.

We do not develop friendly relations with all individuals with whom we interact. We develop friendly relations with those who provide us with some support for our views of ourselves and facilitate performance of our formal roles. Engagement in some voluntary interaction is an indication that we have established a friendly relation.

Friendship relationships necessitate interaction that is more unambiguously voluntary. To indicate to ourselves and others that we have established an intimate, enduring relationship such as friendship, we get involved in activities and situations at times clearly beyond those associated with formal role positions. We plan to continue to associate voluntarily with one another, even if our formal role relationship is dissolved (e.g., through a change of residence or job). Although contacts between individuals may become less voluntary during later stages of friendships because of obligations created by the relationship, the original contacts as friends are voluntary.

SENSE OF UNIQUENESS

A friendly relation lacks the sense of uniqueness there is in friendship. If we had a friendly relation with the occupant of a counterposition, when the former one leaves we generally will try to establish a friendly relation with the new occupant of the position. If we have always had friendly relations with our neighbors or coworkers, we become disconcerted when we cannot establish friendly relations with our new neighbors or coworkers.

Many friendly relations are bound up with one another, so that networks of them are established. These networks often reflect the ties that these relationships have to formal role positions. For example, a secretary may establish friendly relations with the secretaries in the offices surrounding hers and they in turn may form them with the secretaries in the offices surrounding theirs. Thus, a number of individuals are bound up in a complex network of friendly relations, none of which is particularly unique.

In a friendship there is a feeling that the other individual is involved in a special union with one. Since we have few friendships and many friendly relations, each friendship is a unique relationship. In friendships our plans for the future include that particular other, for we do not have a similar relationship with any other.

LEVEL OF INTIMACY

Friendly relations cannot have deep intimacy or personal involvement of a high order. If more intimate information is revealed, the individuals find the relationship has become more like a friendship or a courtship relationship. Friendly relations that endure for some time may attain deeper intimacy than more transient ones, but they do not regularly encompass the intimacy that friendships do. If a deep level of intimacy is reached, individuals are propelled into a different relationship.

Important factors inhibit intimacy in friendly relations. Friendly relation networks tend to inhibit revelation of intimate information, for none of the relationships lends itself to intimacy more than any other and the revelation of information to one individual in the network might lead to its disclosure to a number of individuals. Frequently the situations in which encounters between individuals who have friendly relations take place are not conducive to intimate revelations. People are unlikely to share intimate information with one another if they are in an office, for example.

Although individuals differ in self-revelation and thus in how intimate the content of their relationship is, any particular individual reserves what he feels is most intimate for a few relationships, such as marriage and close friendship (Jourard, 1964, pp. 177–78). Friendships require the revelation of more intimate information (Simmel, 1950, pp. 126–28). Each person feels that the other is joined in a unique relationship with him and is someone with whom he can be intimate. This intimacy is important to friendships, for once a certain level is reached individuals feel bound to one another and frequently seem led to greater revelation and greater involvement. Once an individual has shared intimate knowledge with another, he generally feels he has little to lose by revealing more. And individuals who have formed friendships voluntarily interact with one another in settings more conducive to intimate revelation.

OBLIGATIONS

Sociologists have focused on obligations of occupants of particular positions, but generally they have not considered obligations in various types of interpersonal relationships. McCall and Simmons have noted that when an interpersonal relationship forms, "a person lets himself in for more than he may have bargained for. This seemingly simple action actually entails the recruitment of alter, and of himself, into a fairly inviolable social structure, that once entered, binds both parties in a complex web of obligations and sentiments" (1966, p. 178). Whenever we become involved with others on a personal basis, obligations arise that are above and beyond those associated with the formal positions we occupy.

Obligations are more limited in friendly relations than they are in friendships. For a relationship to be a friendly relation the number and types of interpersonal obligations must be limited, requiring continual effort. If more obligations develop, one or both of the individuals may become disenchanted with the relationship and as a consequence try to destroy it, or alternatively they may let it develop into a friendship or some other intimate relationship. By continuing to interact with another the individual runs the risk that the other individual or third parties may make him feel obligated or act as if he is obligated more than he desires to be. Goffman noted the difficulties in simply making oneself conversationally accessible to others when he stated that even

> words can act as a "relationship wedge"; that is, once an individual has extended to another enough consideration to hear him out for a moment, some kind of bond of mutual obligation is established, which the initiator can use in turn as a basis for still further claims;

once this new extended bond is granted, grudgingly or willingly, still further claims for social or material indulgence can be made (1963a, p. 105).

Individuals in a friendly relation must not let obligations multiply or they soon will no longer have a friendly relation.

Ideally, in friendships obligations are unlimited. Friendships and friendly relations can be distinguished by this expectation and by the fact that friendships actually do encompass more obligations. It is hard to limit obligations, for if it is a "true" friendship, the individuals should want to and will in fact "do anything" for one another. A friend is obligated figuratively if not literally to "give you the shirt off his back." Generally, we do not feel the full weight of the numerous obligations involved in our friendships, because of the affective ties that exist.

In friendly relations we lack the strong affective ties that lead individuals to become deeply involved with one another. If we develop strong sentiments of liking for another person, we form more intimate relationships, such as friendships, with them, and having a friendly relation with them is only a stage in the development of such a relationship. We *maintain* friendly relations with those we do not have strong feelings for and perhaps even dislike somewhat. Often we do not have strong feelings for our coworkers, but we desire to develop a friendly relation with them. We can develop a friendly relation with an individual we dislike if we feel forced to establish some relationship beyond the formal role relationship. For example, if a woman's husband likes another man and develops a friendship with him, she may establish a friendly relation with her husband's friend's wife if she finds herself frequently with her, even if she dislikes her.

Individuals who form friendships have strong feelings of affection for one another. The higher levels of obligation and stronger positive sentiments are causes as well as consequences of the considerable personal involvement in friendship.

Before considering the formation and development of friendly relations and friendships, I shall consider some factors governing the likelihood and nature of the continued voluntary association upon which both are based.

Factors Affecting Bases of Association

Although one person can make friends with numerous individuals and we each have a variety of friends, important factors limit the extent and nature of our voluntary associations with others. The following discussion considers some factors affecting association between various sets of individuals. Since there are so many constraints upon interaction, I make no attempt to enumerate or relate them all. My focus is on the variables of age, sex, and marital status, which are frequently overlooked but play an important role in determining whether people will form a relationship and what type it will be (a friendly relation or a friendship). These factors limit the possibilities of and our desire to pursue interaction with various others.

In studying the effects of demographic factors upon the bases of association, the effects of various norms associated with them becomes our concern, for it is through such norms that these factors affect association. These norms limit what others we are likely to interact with and in what way the interaction will proceed. They tend to set limits upon association within which other variables become crucial in determining particular choices (e.g., close friend). Perhaps future research could ascertain similar norms associated with other classes of variables as well, so that we would better understand normative restrictions upon association and thus limitations upon forming friendships.

The norms associated with the variables of age, sex, and marital status regulate the nature and extent of interaction with various others. I selected these particular variables because they are highly visible but frequently overlooked. Studies of friendship choice generally have not seriously considered these demographic variables, perhaps from oversight of the obvious or because the populations studied typically have been homogeneous in these variables.[3]

3. Examples of studies of homogeneous groups are in Festinger *et al.* (1959) and Newcomb (1961). The effects of one demographic variable, socioeconomic status, on friendship choice have been explored for college students and small communities. The studies have indicated that individuals choose others of similar or adjacent statuses on sociometric measures (Lindzey and Borgatta in Lindzey, 1954, pp. 405–48).

These associated norms seem to be oriented to preventing relationships that *exploit* persons or violate other social values. Although they inhibit friendships when exploitation is very likely, they yet permit the formation of friendly relations. Since prevention of exploitation underlies the norms associated with all three of our variables, the following discussion of them will focus upon this aspect.

The position in this paper is that there are constraints upon association between individuals whose characteristics *might* be conducive to the creation of an exploitative relationship (e.g., the forty-year-old bachelor high school teacher and the teenage boys in his classes). There is always the potential of forming exploitative relationships and of transforming existing relationships into exploitative ones. Since individuals with characteristics conducive to exploitation do interact to some extent, there are pressures upon them to establish only friendly relations at most. (However, even if such persons do interact, they often find it difficult to form an intimate relationship with one another, since in their experience interaction between persons with their characteristics has always been limited.)

It seems, for example, that there is a general expectation that individuals form friendships with others of approximately the same *age*. During the years we are making many close friendships, our role relationships provide us with many opportunities voluntarily to interact with individuals who are our own age. Generally, children's parents allow them to interact only with others of the same age. People of other ages with whom they have the opportunity to interact voluntarily are usually relatives and not considered potential friends. Once a youth has left school, his contacts with people of different ages perhaps increase. However, even then the opportunities for establishing voluntary contacts and intimate relations tend to be restricted to those who are of *approximately* his own age.

This norm is continually reinforcing, for if interaction is limited to those who are similar, then we will learn to find those individuals rewarding (Newcomb, 1956; Lazarsfeld and Merton, 1954). This normative expectation is probably related to several things. First, people of similar ages may tend to have similar interests and to be similar in other respects—certain activities and interests are age related.[4] Another factor is that people of similar ages are frequently similar in resources, so that exploitation is less likely to occur. Thus, a young man should be friendly with his grandmother, but not equally so with other old ladies, unless he is forced to. If individuals of disparate ages become friends, it is often suspected that socially undesirable exploitation is occurring.[5] The younger person may be "extorting" money from the older person or the latter may be "stealing" the younger person's youth.

Sex is another variable that strongly affects the formation of friendships. Except during courtship, men and women are not expected to pursue interaction voluntarily with one another. And then they are not expected to form friendships with one another, but to try to find a marriage partner, thus the assertion that "men and women can be lovers, but never friends."

This expectation could perhaps be based upon similarities of same-sex individuals.[6] Homans (1950, Chaps. 5 and 6) notes the importance of similarity "in some respects" in activities and sentiments to the formation and maintenance of relationships. The question is why do we stress some aspects rather than others. Is it more important that two men share an interest in baseball than that a man and a woman share an interest in cancer research?

This expectation that cross-sex friendships will not be formed is also based upon fears of exploitative or "undesirable" sexual relationships. This fear is particularly apparent when age is considered in conjunction with sex. If individuals of opposite sexes and disparate ages engage in extensive voluntary interaction with one

4. The similarities on which these expectations appear to be based might be a consequence, as well as a cause, of limitation of voluntary interaction to others of approximately the same age. A problem in designing studies of the bases of friendship choice is that people's attitudes tend to become more similar as they interact. For a general discussion of the importance of similar backgrounds and values to interaction, see Homans (1961, pp. 214–19).

5. If an individual violates such norms, he may be labeled as mentally ill. Goffman (1967, pp. 137–48 and 1963a, Chap. 14) has suggested that such labeling is one way we explain and cope with rule violations.

6. Perhaps the distinctive male and female interaction patterns that are referred to are to some extent the result of rather exclusive association with members of their own sex. This exclusive association can lead to and support different rules governing interaction and interactive styles (Bond and Vinacke, 1961; Vinacke, 1959; Argyle, 1967, p. 69).

another, they are generally criticized and gossiped about. Even a courtship relationship between them is undesirable because of the likelihood that it might be exploitative, although the norms regulating the formation of exploitative relationships generally appear somewhat less rigid for courtship relationships, because of our beliefs about love.

There seems to be an expectation that individuals form friendships with individuals who have the same *marital status*. Generally, the expectations concern the broad categories of those currently married and others (single, separated, divorced, or widowed). The restrictions on association by marital status are linked with those associated with sex. Currently married people of either sex are not expected to seek out interaction with people of another marital status, especially if they are of the opposite sex. Perhaps this is one reason for the pressures on marital couples in our society to form friendships with other marital couples. Many bachelors tell stories of how their old friends' wives who were so friendly during their courtship days try to sabotage their friendships once they are married because they feel these relationships threaten their marriages.

It also seems that individuals in any other marital status are expected to associate with those of similar marital status. The single girl is not expected to associate with her old girl friend who is the same age and now divorced, although such normative restrictions are less closely observed now than they apparently were in the past.

These expectations again are based upon similarity of interest to some extent. Married men should associate with other married men who are similarly concerned with keeping the lawn mowed and their wives from straying. The norms tend to stress similarities and thus relationships that support the institution of marriage. The opposite sex associations between people not currently married are tolerated because of the possibilities of marriage. On the whole, such expectations operate to keep individuals in various marital statuses behaving appropriately.

Generally, violations of these norms are not a problem, for we have learned to deprecate the value of such proscribed relationships and would not consider entering them; also, others observe our behavior and try to prevent such relationships from developing.

However, exploitative relationships do occur, whether or not their basis is in differences associated with demographic characteristics. Waller (1938, p. 272), for example, observed courtship and marriage relationships that were exploitative. His "principle of least interest" states that "that person is able to dictate the conditions of association whose interest in the continuation of the affair is least." The more interested individual has less power and may therefore be exploited because the other individual can negotiate an inequitable exchange. Although the "principle of least interest" can be observed operating in many relationships, Homans' principle of distributive justice suggests that individuals find such relationships distasteful (be they the high- or low-power person), since they expect that what they put into a relationship and what they get out of it should be roughly proportional to what the other is putting in and getting out of the relationship. Homans (1961) notes:

> A man in an exchange relationship with another will expect that the rewards of each man will be proportional to his costs—the greater the rewards, the greater the costs—and that the net rewards, or profits, of each man be proportional to his investments—the greater the investments, the greater the profits (p. 232).

It seems that individuals become involved in inequitable relationships because they desire the relationship more than they do justice in the current situation.

Organizational Constraints on Association

Organizations provide bases of association that sometimes conflict with the normative expectations associated with these demographic variables. In many organizations people become deeply involved in (e.g., work organizations, social movements, religious organizations), individuals who share many interests and activities are brought into extensive contact. They may be of varying ages, both sexes, and every marital status. Only work organizations are discussed here, since we are perhaps most familiar with the effects of such organizational membership upon association.

Work organizations frequently try formally and informally to regulate the development of intimate relationships between individuals occupying various formal positions. These organizations are concerned with exploitative, "least interest" relationships based on power differentials resulting from formal positions in the organization. Usually, organizational strictures prohibit the formation of friendships by individuals within the organization except for those who hold equal status positions. Thus, there are norms prohibiting the formation of friendships between workers and supervisors.

The restrictions on friendship formation imposed by work organizations do not limit individuals on the same basis as the demographic variables. In such organizations members with differing demographic characteristics may form friendships if they comply with the *organization's* restrictions. However, the *individuals* in the organization tend to make matters difficult for such friendships because they support the norms associated with the demographic characteristics. The following discussion considers how relationships that conflict with the norms associated with the demographic variables develop in these organizations.

It is possible for individuals in these organizations of different age, sex, and/or marital status to form friendships if they hold equivalent positions in the organization. They frequently have similar interests from their involvement in the organization. They find it economical to establish interpersonal relationships with others in the organization, both because they do not have much time for outside relationships, and because of the considerable rewards obtainable from those people with similar interests. Demographically disparate persons in an organization may form at least a quasi-respectable friendship if others recognize that they are frequently thrown together and share organizational interests. However, there is still normative preference for mere friendly relations between such individuals.

The discussion above of the norms associated with some selected demographic variables indicates that the voluntary interaction between individuals, when exploitation is likely, is normatively restricted, and friendly relations are encouraged at the expense of friendship. It also brings out the considerable influence the norms exert upon our associations with other—whether or not we are aware of them.

Our society is possibly in a transitional state. In the past relationships between individuals with disparate demographic characteristics were undesirable and unlikely. Now, they are more likely but still not desirable. Friendly relations provide a means for these individuals to get satisfaction from associating with one another while not becoming involved in friendships. The participation of individuals in organizations that provide them with extensive contact with individuals of disparate characteristics challenges norms prohibiting friendship.

Processes of Friendship Formation and Development

Individuals who form friendship relationships have been brought into contact with one another through a formal role relationship. If a friendship forms between such individuals, each must *perceive* that the other is interested in forming a relationship and each must *decide* that he wants that type of relationship. It is relatively easy and natural for a friendly relation to develop between individuals who have a formal role relationship because of the rules of civil interaction. Once they have formed a friendly relation, they decide whether or not to form a friendship. The following discussion considers the processes whereby friendships are developed from friendly relations.

REWARD-COST EXPLORATION

Thibaut and Kelley (1959, pp. 65–6) have suggested that initially individuals try to gather two types of information about the rewards and costs possible in a relationship. First, individuals engage in a process of "tentative exploration" to ascertain as much as possible about the reward-cost structure of a relationship with the other. As the term exploration suggests, an individual does not and cannot find out about all the rewards and costs possible. The individual must content himself with trying to make a more or less adequate survey of currently available rewards and costs. Some are highly visible, others are not; some are more important than others. An individual's exploration is probably most adequate for the most visible rewards and costs and for those that are most important to him at that time. Second, the individual tries to "forecast trends" in his outcomes, particularly their stability. The individual tries to consider the effects of various events upon the outcomes that he believes are or will be available.

To some extent we continue to explore potential rewards and costs and test their stability throughout the lifetime of a relationship. Exploration is particularly important at first, however, for the results of it determine the fate of the potential relationship (Thibaut and Kelley, 1959, pp. 19–21). Individuals must make inferences about what relationship is possible and what is possible in that relationship on the basis of information gathered by the rather inadequate means available for tentative exploration. If the outcomes do not seem "good" and/or stable at first, a person loses interest in further exploration and the development of a relationship.

CIVIL INTERACTION AS A BARRIER TO EXPLORATION

When people interact with one another, they are governed by sets of norms or rules. The general rules that routinely make possible interaction between various people in diverse situations have been extensively explored by Goffman (1963a; 1961, pp. 17–81). While the rules of civil interaction make it possible for individuals to cope with one another with a minimum of effort, they also serve as a barrier to exploration.

These rules make it difficult to ascertain what particular rewards and costs are available in a relationship with a specific individual. For example, at a party people feel constrained to maintain focus upon what the individual with whom they are engaged is saying and to make some show of interest in it. Rules of polite conduct forbid saying "I'm not interested in that" and simply suggesting topics until a truly mutually agreeable one is found or until it is decided on the basis of this exploration that there is no point in interacting with one another.

Although civil interaction is a barrier to exploration, it is profitable for us to engage in it. The rules are important to our maintenance of our views of ourselves during the multitude of exchanges we have with others. In general, we are expected to accept the "faces" we project to one another (Goffman, 1967, pp. 5–47). Each is expected to present a reasonable face, and the others are constrained to help him establish, maintain, or recover it if necessary. Since most of us in our daily rounds encounter others who adhere to the same set of rules, we can interact with a minimum of effort by bringing into play the rules applicable to the situation, and we can thus gain some support for our views of ourselves.[7]

These rules suggest that it is generally profitable for us to establish friendly relations with those our formal role relationships bring us into contact with, for they can provide us with support for our views of ourselves. However, the polite responses of these individuals do not provide us with deep support for many of our faces nor support for the unique faces that we feel uncertain about presenting to such individuals—support that we can obtain in intimate relationships such as friendship.

Polite, stereotyped forms of behavior are low-cost, low-gain behavior. In relation to the process of reward-cost exploration, Thibaut and Kelley (1959) note, "It may be readily seen that such inhibited and stereotyped behavior leads both to a reduction of sample size and to a biasing of the sample of outcome" (p. 68). Such behavior makes interaction easy, but it makes the formation of a unique relationship difficult.

THE LINE AS A BARRIER TO EXPLORATION

The stereotyped "line" is frequently useful during exploratory interaction, for it facilitates further exploration and does not commit the person to a relationship. Waller (1938, pp. 262–3) considers the difficulties of ascertaining the reward and cost structure in a potential courtship relationship because of the standard use of such highly conventionalized and exaggerated forms of speech. The "line" is an accepted means by which males and females conceal their "true" feelings about each other and the type of relationship they desire. Waller suggests that the use of the line leads to a

---

7. Goffman has suggested that the rules he has uncovered provide guidelines for middle class American society and that other groups may have different rules.

state of "pluralistic ignorance," in which each individual is uncertain of the actual attitudes of the other. Each uses the line in order not to reveal his true feelings and consequently each is uncertain of the other's feelings because the other uses the line.

The use of the line by an individual we are interacting with is a barrier to ascertaining what he means, what type of relationship he desires, and what kinds of rewards and costs would be encountered in a relationship with him. When we feel the other is giving us a line, we are somewhat uncertain of how he feels about us. Perhaps even more problematic is our ability to ascertain whether it is a line we are receiving, for our responses generally are considerably different depending upon whether it is or not. (In courtship relationships, such as Waller studied, individuals to some extent expect that the other is giving them a line. In other situations our expectations are not so clear.) We all have known the discomfort that results from extending a line to another and finding that he takes it seriously, as well as the agony of trying to decide if the other guy is feeding us a line.

MOVES TOWARD FRIENDSHIP

In distinguishing friendly relations from friendship, we noted that in friendships individuals engage in activities and in situations at times beyond those required by their formal roles. In forming a friendship individuals must "move" away from what is required to what is clearly voluntary.[8]

For this movement to occur, one must make an initial move to indicate that he desires a change in the relationship.[9] Once he makes a move that could be interpreted as a desire to step outside of the established role relationship, the other must decide what led to the act, what motivated it.

The first decision is whether the move perceived as an overture of friendship was indeed a deliberate sign (indication) that the other desired to change the relationship. If a fellow worker buys a man a drink after work or if a neighbor invites him over for the

8. A discussion of "moves" to initiate encounters in which their simultaneity is stressed is presented by Goffman (1963a, pp. 91–2).

9. Waller (1938, p. 275) suggests that one individual must take the lead in instigating movement through the stages and that the individual's initiative reflects his greater involvement in the relationship.

evening, he must decide what it means in terms of the future, whether it is motivated by a desire for a change in their relationship. The various moves made and how they are responded to determine whether a friendship will be formed.

It is easier to form friendships with people of similar social background, status, and interest, because it is easier to interpret one another's moves. If two people are governed by the same general set of social norms, it is from past experience easier to interpret their moves (or at least the individual usually feels more confident about doing so (Thibaut and Kelley, 1959, p. 66). When there are power and status differences, it is more difficult to ascertain the meaning of what was done. Perhaps when there are such differences the person lower in power or status will wait for the other to initiate the change. And the lower person would be more uncertain about whether what could be interpreted as an act motivated by a desire for change means there is a desire for a changed relationship. Uncertainty about moves can thus support the norms associated with demographic characteristics.

In trying to interpret the moves of another, we place great weight on what could be considered unusual moves. Jones and Davis (1965, pp. 219–66) have suggested that when we are trying to ascertain the dispositions underlying a particular act, we feel more confident about attributions concerning the other when the act has extreme effects, when there are unique effects, and/or when the effects are low in social desirability. The person trying to interpret others' acts must decide whether they were moves or not, and what they suggest for the future of the relationship, before he can decide what to do. Men spend a great deal of time pondering these moves.

If someone is uncertain whether what he took as an indication of desire for an altered basis of interaction (a desire for a higher level of intimacy and/or a movement toward greater involvement) was one or not, he can wait to see if another sign is profered that will more clearly indicate how things stand. However, the person who made the move will be trying to see how he responds or fails to respond. The uncertainty felt about forming relationships and the contradictory feelings about the rewards and costs in relationships once formed make each individual sensitive to the possible implications of his response (or nonresponse) to what *might* have been a move by the other and alert to what might be a response of the other to a move of his.

There is the risk of considerable cost, for some individuals at least, in profering an offer of friendship or suggesting a change in the relationship, when the other is not interested in a relationship of that sort at that time. Consequently, many moves are tentative and deliberately ambiguous. We do not ask others if they will be our friends; we try to indicate that *perhaps* we are interested in forming a friendship with them.

Tentative and ambiguous moves make it possible to avoid incurring several types of costs. If a move is tentative, the individual may prevent an outright rejection, which might destroy the possibilities of the relationship ever becoming what he desires. If a move is tentative and ambiguous it is difficult to reject openly the possibility of changing the relationship, for there is considerable cost if that was not what the move meant. Since an outright rejection is an unlikely response, the individual can make a move again in the future.

Yet there is always the possibility that there may be an outright rejection, however unlikely it may be. An individual who makes a move can save face if his suggestion is spurned by denying that he intended to make a move or by denying that *that* was what his move meant. This is perhaps most easily observed in courtship relationships. Despite our romantic conceptions of marriage proposals, proposing marriage is frequently a very tentative process in which an offer is never formally extended. A man makes a number of moves and tries to "read" the woman's reactions to each of them. Generally, each move is successively less ambiguous. However, many a woman who has tried to smooth a rejection has been confronted by a denial that the offer was ever extended. Thus, individuals can save face in their own eyes, if not in those of others, if they avoid forthright declarations and rely on moves open to more than one interpretation.

Also, we are cautious in the moves we make, for they may destroy the current relationship. When an individual makes a move that the other person takes to signify a desire to change the relationship that other does not desire changed at that time or in the future, other may feel it best to break off the current relationship and foreclose the possibilities of undesired developments. When we are dealing with individuals who differ from us in status and power, we are especially cautious in our moves. Goffman (1963a) has noted the tentative nature of moves to establish an encounter when there is such uncertainty. For example,

> when the individual is socially subordinated to the one to whom he is about to initiate an encounter overture, he may be required to use a minimal sign so that the superior can easily continue to overlook it, or can respond to it at his own convenience (p. 191).

Thus, we are cautious about moves when we are uncertain of what effects they will have upon the formal role relationship and/or uncertain if they will be acceptable considering the nature of the formal role relationship.

Finally, the information communicated through moves is unclear, for when an individual makes one he may be uncertain whether he wants to initiate a change in the relationship. An individual can "pretend," act as if they were not moves, if he changes his mind about desiring to alter the relationship. We are perhaps most familiar with this switch when a person reneges because he feels that the other's response to his move indicates a more radical or rapid change than he had envisioned.

For a friendly relation to become a friendship, individuals must make the appropriate moves at the right time. We have all become involved in relationships with individuals whom we did not particularly care for when we first met them. Those who eventually become our friends and lovers are sometimes people we initially did not care whether we ever saw again. If the other individual makes the critical moves, takes the risk of incurring greater costs, and things go well, we can be drawn into relationships we originally had no interest in. However, these moves have to occur at propitious times, when we feel that we can manipulate our involvements in other relationships to permit us to enter into new ones.

We generally feel that invitations to, or tacit assumptions of, future engagement in voluntary activities are moves that can be interpreted. The initiation of further interaction is viewed as a sign of attraction. In a courtship relationship, the normative expectation is that the male will initiate further interaction, if he is attracted to the female.[10] If she accepts, it is generally expected that she views him favorably. During courtship the frequency with which individuals seek out one another and the amount of time they spend with one another are indicators of the progress of the relationship. It seems that we similarly assess engagement in voluntary interaction when attempting to ascertain attraction in other relationships as well. Common understanding of the possible effects of such interaction upon the relationship is perhaps greatest in courtships. Other persons play an important role in these understandings, for they teach individuals various moves and their meanings and help the individual to interpret others' moves. During courtship a young woman's friends spend many hours helping her interpret passing remarks made by the young man.

When we first interact with others, we are always to some extent concerned with the possibilities available for forming various relationships. We sample rewards and costs and try to ascertain the other's motives. However, while we are sampling we continue to interact with one another, and frequently it is difficult to "hold off" the formation of a friendship until we have acquired enough information about the reward-cost structure. We have made moves toward the formation of a relationship *simply by continuing our exploration.* As a consequence, people remark about a new neighbor's invitation to dinner that they "don't want to get *that* started," for they recognize the possible ramifications of accepting one invitation. Thus, individuals can get "locked into" relationships while they are still trying to decide whether they want to form one.

Once a friendship has been formed, the individuals involved frequently seem to accept as "natural" or inevitable that they should be friends. People perceive one another as similar and appropriate. However, this comes in part from the interaction they have engaged in with one another, for individuals tend to become more similar "in some respects" in their sentiments and activities

10. Although in some cases the male is not attracted to the female even though he initiates further interaction, particularly as the relationship progresses, the male's initiation of further interaction is still the common yardstick used to measure attraction.

with increased interaction (Homans, 1961, p. 120). Feeling that they are similar and that the development of their friendship was "natural" creates bonds between individuals that further the development and maintenance of the relationship.

Friendship Development and Maintenance

We experience ambivalence not only in forming relationships but also throughout their lifetime because of changes in and uncertainty about their relative profitability. Ambivalence represents the conflicting feelings that accompany thoughtful reflection on involvement in a relationship. As Thibaut and Kelley (1959) have noted:

> to enter a new relationship is to abandon an old adaptation—an earlier relationship or state of independence. Some degree of conflict may be inevitable between putting on the new and putting off the old (p. 66).

At times it is brought home to each individual in a relationship that they have bound themselves to another person, that they are dependent upon that person, and that there are considerable costs in the relationship as well as rewards. Ambivalence occurs particularly in the early stages of a relationship. However, it can occur at other points, for if a relationship is transformed the individuals generally have to readapt to some extent.

Our frequent inability to predict or control the direction of relationships makes us wary of entering into them. We have all been involved in relationships that turned out differently than we had expected. Thus, we cannot allow our friendly relations to stray too far from the basis upon which they were formed without their becoming a different type of relationship. Many changes are gradual, and sometimes changes seem to nullify one another, so that a friendship may *appear* to be relatively unchanged for a number of years. Relationships can change without the full awareness of the individuals involved, just as they can form without their full awareness.[11] We can become involved with one another

11. Relationships can be transformed, as Strauss (1959, pp. 44–88) has indicated identities are transformed.

in a type of relationship that one or both of us did not desire or expect to form.

It is easy to start a friendship but not easy, or even in many cases possible, to keep it within the desired bounds, to destroy it, or to make it what it once was. We may drift in and out of friendly relations; however, we do not do the same with friendships. We do not invest much in friendly relations, in order that we can enter and leave them more easily than we can friendships. Many friendships are maintained even though one or both of the individuals feel that they would like to dissolve it. Often we continue with an eye to the day when we will be able "gracefully" to become less involved in the relationship (e.g., by graduating, changing jobs, or moving from the neighborhood). The sense of relief when we can gracefully escape from some of the demands of a friendship has been experienced by most.

By gracefully withdrawing from a relationship, it is possible for us to profit still from seeing one another and to keep from losing all that we have invested in that relationship. Thus, we often look forward to seeing for a brief while those friends we have withdrawn from.

Events are continually occurring that affect the relationship. These events need not be crises or particularly marked off in any way. Many are external to the relationship. For example, a new individual profering an offer of friendship to one member of a relationship can alter his comparison level for alternatives and affect the bargains he will be content with within the relationship. Friendly relations are perhaps more subject to one particular set of external events than are friendships. That is, since friendly relations are closely tied to formal positions and roles, they are affected significantly by changes in them. A friendship requires that one build a substantial relationship on other bases, so that it will persist even if the formal role relationship is dissolved.

Events that occur (or do not occur) bring the current functioning of the relationship into question. These events, which often are not designed by either individual, can threaten the very foundations of a relationship, as well as the everyday working agreements. However, relationships do survive a wide variety of events, partly because of the mechanisms that become operative when individuals form a relationship. Once relationships are formed, some mechanisms operate to keep us in the relationship, to make us behave properly as a member of the relationship, while other mechanisms (sometimes the same ones) tend to propel us into deeper involvement with the other individual.

MECHANISMS OF INVOLVEMENT

The general *norm of reciprocity* that Gouldner (1960) has suggested operates in American society is one of these mechanisms of involvement. The norm of reciprocity refers to the expectation that once a person does something for another individual, the latter will feel constrained to reciprocate. Generally, to reciprocate the individuals must interact with one another again, thus providing a basis for the development and maintenance of relationships.

In a similar vein, Simmel (1950, pp. 379–95) notes the importance of *gratitude* and *faithfulness* to the maintenance of relationships. Individuals feel gratitude when others do something for them. Gratitude operates as a mechanism holding men in their relationships, for the individual feels that he can never repay the original gesture which was given "freely." Thus, the concept of gratitude suggests something more than the norm of reciprocity does. The gratitude we feel toward the person who incurs the risk of making moves critical to the development of a friendship cannot be dissolved by an act of repayment. (It is interesting to note the frequency with which each individual in a friendship perceives that the other individual was "responsible" for the formation of their friendship because he offered such a rewarding "deal" that it would have been foolish to turn him down. Perhaps each of us tends selectively to perceive the other individual as having made these moves.) Also, individuals develop faithfulness to relationships, which serves to maintain the relationship, even if the original motive for forming the relationship no longer remains. Simmel (1950) notes:

> Every beginning relationship is accompanied by a specific feeling, interest, impulse, directed toward it by its participants. If the relation continues, there develops a particular feeling in interaction with this continuance—or, better, often though not always, the original psychic states change into a particular form which we call faithfulness. It is

a psychological reservoir, as it were, an over-all or unitary mold for the most varied interests, affects, and motives of reciprocal bonds. . . . what I mean is that faithfulness itself is a specific psychic state, which is directed toward the continuance of the relation as such, independently of any particular affective or volitional elements that sustain the content of the relationship (p. 381).

Since individuals vary in their interest and involvement in a relationship from one another and over time, the feeling of faithfulness is important to maintaining a relationship.

Another mechanism important to the development and maintenance of a relationship is *commitment.* Commitment is the process whereby individuals accumulate obligations to one another over time. People try to extract commitment from one another, for then they feel assured that they will regularly receive the outcomes that attracted them to the relationship—that there will be stability in their rewards and costs. When an individual is "trading in futures," he is frequently making investments in an attempt to procure such commitments (McCall and Simmons, 1966, p. 179). If people try to avoid becoming involved in the complex web of obligations and sentiments associated with an interpersonal relationship such as friendship, they limit their investments and commitments and try to convince the other individual also to limit his.

THIRD PARTIES

Our idealized conceptions of intimate dyadic relationships of course exclude other people. When we are forming such relationships, we frequently try quite openly to exclude others. This is perhaps one characteristic of what has been termed the "honeymoon" period in relationships. Thus, at first we rather exclusively associate with a new friend or lover. However, others with whom we have relationships eventually remind us of our obligations to them, and we ourselves desire to engage in some of our treasured activities with them. Our attempts to fit together our various relationships provide many opportunities for others to influence any one of our relationships.

Third parties can exert pressures that tend to develop, arrest, maintain, and dissolve our relationships. A friendly relation is the type of relationship we form with many others. It is also a stage in the development of a friendship. Others can affect whether a relationship remains a friendly relation or develops into a friendship. First, by reminding individuals of the norms associated with the demographic variables, others can help arrest relationships between those with disparate demographic characteristics at the friendly relations stage. Since others frequently can observe the moves that individuals make, they can affect the development of the relationship whether the individuals involved desire them to or not. For example, if others observe a relationship and conclude that it is a friendship, they can treat the individuals as if they were friends. This response can further the development of the relationship and, if nothing else, make it more difficult to dissolve or to maintain it as it once was.

Waller (1938) noted in his examination of courtship relationships that they pass through successive stages because of impulses within the individuals (e.g. their desires and interests) and outside pressures. For,

> As the process unfolds, each person becomes increasingly committed in his own eyes and those of others to the completed act, and at the same time his impulses are increasingly stirred up (p. 259).

We are most familiar with the successive stages and with the influence of others on passage through them in the case of courtship relationships. It seems that some such stages also occur in other relationships.

And like courtships, other relationships can be broken off or arrested at various stages, and most are. Unfortunately, we have failed to differentiate the various stages of relationships such as friendship, so that we are less aware of them here than in the case of courtship.

NORMS OF PROPRIETY

Norms of propriety for friends are also important to the development and maintenance of friendships. In intimate relationships such as friendship, individuals violate norms of civil interaction—friendship formation is contingent upon revelation of one's "true" self and that self can be revealed only by violating these norms.[12]

12. See the papers by Denzin and Suttles in this volume.

Thus, individuals will reveal deviant information about themselves or engage in deviant activity with one another. As individuals interact more with one another, they frequently feel constrained to reveal more about themselves, and situations arise in which more about themselves is directly revealed. To some extent such relationships seem to be held together by the threat of exposing information that the individuals have about one another, as well as by the reward of having someone to some extent accept this revelation of personal deviance.

Individuals in an intimate relationship have many opportunities to create rewards and/or costs for one another by means of the information each has learned about the other. In a friendly relation individuals attempt to prevent much information that is not common knowledge from becoming available. First, if an individual reveals intimate information about himself to the other, it may be construed as a "move" indicating a desire for a friendship. Consequently, if a person does not want to form a friendship, he will be careful about revealing information. Second, there is considerable risk involved in bringing such information into a friendly relation, for individuals in friendly relations are not as bound by the norms that protect revelations in friendships. As a result, individuals in friendly relations usually do not reap the rewards of revealing intimate or deviant information nor do they risk the costs, for the revelation of such information to one another does not often occur.

In a friendship, individuals have secret information about one another, but they are bound by the norms of propriety for friends not to reveal it. If an individual reveals such information, the individual he has formed the relationship with can in turn divulge information about him or he can alter or destroy their relationship. Also, third parties do not expect an individual seriously or frequently to violate the norms governing revelation of secrets about friends. These others can punish an individual if he does—for example, by refusing to associate with him. In addition, in an established relationship an individual's reputation is linked with the others, so that discrediting information about the other is frequently damaging to himself as well. To some extent we judge a man by his friends, so that it does not pay a man to discredit them.

Character of Negotiation Within a Stable Relationship

Individuals in relationships are involved in social exchange with one another. Homans (1961) has proposed that individuals expect equity in their exchanges with one another. The expectations of equity and other aspects of social exchange, however, operate differently in friendships and friendly relations. The following discussion focuses on negotiation within friendships.

In interpersonal relationships individuals do not demand distributive justice in every encounter. By focusing upon the exchange that occurs in particular encounters one can get a distorted view of the exchange that occurs in a friendship, for individuals in such relationships have "standing accounts" with one another. Experimental evidence suggests that "the history of exchanges between participants in a social relationship may be extensive enough firmly to establish evaluative parity as a common definition relatively impervious to temporary disruptions in exchange balance." (Weinstein, et al, 1969, p. 11). In a friendship individuals can draw on past credits and also trade in futures without disrupting the sense of balanced exchange. Thus, in an enduring relationship such as friendship, past experiences and possibilities for the future as well as the current situation affect the exchange in an encounter.

On the other hand, friendly relations emphasize parity in encounters. When individuals establish a friendly relation, they are oriented to the present situation with the other, rather than to the past or future. Individuals in a friendly relation are generally not committed to extensive future relations. They try to avoid trading in futures because it commits them in the future and can lead to the development of a different type of relationship (e.g., a friendship).

People are oriented to attaining the highest possible outcomes in their relationships. As a consequence, they continually negotiate within their relationships to maximize their outcomes. Since an individual does not always feel "free" to end an unprofitable relationship because of the bonds that have been created or the lack of better opportunities, he tries optimally to renegotiate the bargains he has struck in this and his other relationships. Negotiation can result in considerable transformation of a relationship, so that, a friendly relation may become a friendship or a friendship may develop into a love affair. Since negotiation seems to be a continual process within relationships, there is always the possibility that relationships will change.

The social exchange concepts of comparison level and comparison level for alternatives (Thibaut and Kelley, 1959), as well as the principle of distributive justice (Homans, 1961), suggest that individuals are continually evaluating their rewards and costs in a relationship and comparing them with their expectations, with what they might receive in alternative relationships, and with what is received by others. The negotiation within relationships is a consequence of this continual evaluation and comparison.

TESTING THE RELATIONSHIP

First, we shall consider the "testing" characteristic of negotiation within relationships. Once a relationship is formed, individuals are concerned about the stability of rewards and costs in the relationship. As a consequence, people periodically feel the need to assert themselves, so that their partners remember their obligations.

> The longer the sequence of Ego's conforming actions, the more likely is Alter to take Ego's conformity for granted, the less appreciative Alter will feel and the less propensity he will have to reward and reciprocate Alter's conforming action (Gouldner, 1959, p. 424).

Individuals check to see if the other is "holding up his end." In terms of the moves that individuals make in a relationship, testing is a means for ascertaining how similar each person's view of the relationship is. A relationship may be transformed as well as maintained by such testing.

Waller noted in his observations of courtship relationships that individuals frequently recognize that they have become more involved in the relationship but fear that the other individual has maintained his original level of involvement (Thibaut and Kelley, 1959, pp. 114–15). He proposes that both individuals frequently have this perception, and tension resulting from their perceptions may result in quarrels. At such times the involvement of each in the relationship is tested. If the individuals do not successfully manage these tensions, the relationship may be broken off or arrested at that level.

In our friendships we sometimes feel that we are becoming dependent upon another individual and are not sure how involved he is in the relationship. We will frequently initiate incidents to test his involvement. Often we seem to test our relationships by making the other individual choose between meeting our demands and those of another relationship. If he makes the wrong move, in some cases we try to bring him into line. If we cannot, we often try to lessen our involvement in the relationship. On the other hand, if he makes the right move (choice), we will perhaps try to incorporate more into the relationship. In the following discussion we shall consider the conflict that occurs as well as the various means of its resolution.

The intimacy and intensity of friendship relationships leaves them particularly prone to conflict (Waller, 1938, p. 330). In friendships there can be greater conflict than in friendly relations because of the greater ability of individuals in such relationships to make demands upon one another and to resist them. In friendly relations individuals are less likely to become involved in the conflicts that result from intense, highly intimate relationships with others.

To clarify further the differences in negotiation in friendships and friendly relations, we shall consider the effects of issues upon which individuals hold conflicting views. In any relationship there are issues upon which each of the individuals hold divergent views, whether it be the use of drugs or Japanese art. Usually we do not feel the need to resolve these differences, so long as they are not over issues central to the relationship.

In friendly relations issues of conflict are avoided. Often individuals in a friendly relation invoke the rules of civil interaction; they set up narrow boundaries about what is permitted in the relationship to avoid conflicts over many issues. Political discussion in one friendly relation may be off limits, off color jokes in another. Since we have many friendly relations, individuals involved in a friendly relation can incorporate various things not suitable in one friendly relation into their other relationships. If open conflict occurs in a friendly relation, it is perhaps more likely to lead to

severing the relationship than if such conflict occurs in a friendship. We try to avoid conflict in a friendly relation, for it may
bring formal role relationships into play, threatening the existence
of the voluntary relationship.

Individuals frequently test a relationship such as friendship by
reopening or introducing issues of conflict. Individuals in friendships conduct sustained hostilities, "cold wars," with one another
on issues more or less important to them and more or less central
to their relationships. Conflict exists in all relationships to some
extent at all times.[13] If one individual views an issue as central to
the relationship, the hostilities probably are greater and the possibilities that the relationship will be transformed are also greater.

There are a number of maneuvers individuals can use to try to
change the other's position. An individual can attempt to influence
the other by attacking him, by indicating that his own position is
not changed, or by threatening to expose secret knowledge about
him. Also, he can try to influence the other by increasing the other's rewards. If he is not successful in influencing the other, he
can try to withdraw to some extent from the relationship.

WITHDRAWING FROM A RELATIONSHIP

A man may find that the outcomes he is achieving in a relationship
are not what he feels he should be achieving based on his comparison level for alternatives. Costs may be unexpected or greater
than anticipated, and expected rewards may not materialize or
may be unstable.

If one cannot induce or coerce the other into rectifying the situation, he may to some extent withdraw from the relationship.
Someone who is not receiving the expected support for a highly
valued role-identity may bring it into the relationship less and less
and seek to change another existing relationship or to form a new
one in which he will get support for it. If he does so, the friendship
can be seriously threatened, for he is likely to become less involved
in it and more involved in the supportive relationship, since it
more closely provides him with what he feels he deserves.

13. We sometimes overlook this conflict because of our focus on violent
quarrels. Many women quietly leave their husbands because of their failures
in "cold wars" rather than because of violent quarreling.

To narrow or contract a friendship, a person needs the cooperation of the other. When he tries to contract a relationship, he may find the other holding him to old bargains. Since we frequently do not want to destroy the relationship, we may try to convince the other that we are not that rewarding to him, that he will be "better off" if he becomes more involved with someone else, so that he will not hold us to the old bargains. Frequently we try to lessen "gracefully" our involvement in friendships. We feel we must be careful so that we do not destroy the relationship and lose all that we have invested in it.

EXPANDING THE RELATIONSHIP

Another way of transforming a relationship is *adding* something new. A person may try to incorporate more of what he values into a profitable relationship. We feel a strain toward totality in our interpersonal relationships because of our desire for greater reward and our fear that the other will uncover secrets, which will harm our relationship.

> Personal economy dictates that we try to get as much as possible out of each of our relationships, to include as much of ourselves as is profitable. We must try to cultivate, as well as merely to preserve our various relationships (McCall and Simmons, 1966, p. 196).

This strain is important in developing a friendship from a friendly relation.

When we first form relationships, we include few things (e.g., our more common role-identities) and keep many secrets. There is a tendency over time, however, to incorporate more in them if they have been going well. If in comparing rewards and costs, we decide it would be profitable to introduce some new aspect, we often will. The ambivalence described earlier occurs when individuals are uncertain, as they sometimes are, about whether they are or are not willing to become more involved. People who desire to maintain friendly relations try to resist the strain toward totality. They become embarrassed or irritated when the other person tries to bring more into the relationship, for such behavior is interpreted as a "move" signaling a desire for change in the relationship.

In negotiations within stable relationships, the influence of third parties must also be considered, for they can do much to shape the bargains that are struck.

THIRD PARTIES AND RELATIONSHIP NEGOTIATION

Others not only influence the formation and development of relationships, they influence the negotiations that occur between individuals in a stable relationship (Goode, 1960). Our various relationships influence negotiation within any one relationship. The bargains we make in each relationship play a role in all. In negotiation in any relationship the individual is trying to maximize his profits in that relationship and in general, since he can only do so many things. Second, the others with whom we are involved in relationships may more directly try to influence our other relationships by criticizing the bargains we have hammered out in them. Some others may feel it their duty to keep relationships from being exploitative. Some may feel a bargain is threatening if it is exploitative, for we may subsequently try to exploit them (e.g., drive a harder bargain or perform less well).

It is difficult for individuals to conceal exploitative exchanges from others. McCall and Simmons (1966) note that the bargains in interpersonal relationships are visible to all. Thus,

> In the interpersonal relationship, in which there is no one else to hide behind or to use as a distraction, the revered norms of reciprocity in exchange, of distributive justice, can be seen to work unimpeded by other persons. . . . The purity of reciprocity entails only that such imbalances are much more difficult to conceal or legitimate than they are in more complex social structures (p. 178).

Since others can observe bargains in relationships, they may draw conclusions about the purity of reciprocity and try to influence the individuals if they feel negotiation has been exploitative. Unfortunately, many important things that individuals exchange, such as support for highly prized but little known role-identities, often are not apparent to others.

Some third parties may be more influential than others. The degree of concern the third party feels and the amount of pressure he can exert determines his influence. If an individual is deeply involved with third parties, they can coerce him by threatening to suspend or alter their relationships with him.

Summary and Conclusions

Friendly relations are a type of relationship prevalent today. Friendly relations occur more frequently than friendships and we often prefer them to more intense friendship relationships, although friendly relations may be a stage in friendship development. A friendly relation is a voluntary relation, but it is closely tied to the individuals' formal role relationship. Frequently, in the course of being "sociable" with our neighbors or coworkers we establish a friendly relation. To form a friendship, we must move beyond the formal role relationship and the friendly relation. We must clearly establish the voluntary nature of our interaction, recognize the uniqueness of the relationship, develop a high level of intimacy, and become involved in a network of obligations.

Society lacks terminological distinctions. We call "friends" people with whom we do little more than exchange "good mornings," members of our high school or college sets, some of our colleagues, and various and sundry others. Although there are some terms (such as "acquaintance") that could be used to make a distinction, they are not commonly used. Consequently, a person can draw undesired attention to the distinction he may want to make casually in the course of a conversation. It would generally be considered impolite to refer to someone with whom we have a friendly relation as a mere acquaintance and to someone else as a friend. Also, such distinctions are perhaps not made in order not to foreclose the possibilities of developing a friendship in the future. Distinguishing a person as an acquaintance could be interpreted as a move blocking the development of a friendship.

Empirical research has frequently confused these two types of relationship, probably because of the everyday lack of distinction between them and the fact that a friendly relation is a stage in the development of a friendship. If we are to find out more about various categories of relationships and the way we distribute our time among them, we must distinguish similar but distinctive types.

To understand the prevalence of friendly relations, we must investigate their desirability and the pressures against friendship formation between individuals.

It has been hypothesized that people find friendly relations desirable because they facilitate their performance of their formal roles, provide some minimum support for their views of themselves, and do not involve much cost. An individual can enter into a number of friendly relations that will assist him in his daily rounds, while he can only enter into a few friendships.

Certainly third parties and norms promote the maintenance of friendly relations between many individuals and tend to prohibit the formation of friendships between them. In this paper the role of such norms and the influence of third parties have been explored to some extent.

It would be of interest to explore how open people are to friendship at various points in the life cycle. If throughout our lives commitments build up and we seldom dissolve friendships or other intimate relationships in which we have heavily invested, we undoubtedly must be less open to friendships as we grow older. We need to know more about the dissolution of relationships and the effects of existing commitments on the formation of new relationships. If we most frequently wait for opportunities when we can gracefully lessen our involvement in a relationship, then we are generally less open, less free, to form friendships most of the time.

A Collaborative Overview
of Social Relationships

In this final chapter we collaboratively review our papers in an endeavor to delineate what we feel are important and (to us at least) surprising convergences, including common omissions, in our individual analyses of social relationships. It is not our intention to submerge the substantial differences among us of emphasis and subsequent direction in our different formulations of these common themes.

The Nature of Social Relationships

The clearest and most basic convergences in our papers extend across four major points—the definition of social relationships, the range of relationships, their character as social organizations, and the role of deviance.

DEFINITION OF SOCIAL RELATIONSHIPS

First, all five papers clearly construe a social relationship as being between two individuals—*not* between two roles or two arbitrary members of some social categories. Second, the emphasis is upon the substantial probability of recurring interaction between the two persons if a social relationship between them is asserted. Third, considerable point is made of the members' symbolization or recognition of the relationship and this probability of recurring interaction. Fourth, all five papers emphasize that this probability is based on the fit between the members' roles and/or selves.

The definition of social relationship that emerges from our work is *a symbolically recognized probability of recurring interaction between two persons as distinctive individuals, based on some functional fit between their respective roles and/or selves.*

THE RANGE OF SOCIAL RELATIONSHIPS

Given such a conception of social relationships, it is apparent to us that the empirical range or variety of relationships even within a single society is extremely wide, as a function in turn of the numerous types of possible functional fit, the great range of social roles, and the virtually innumerable shapes of social selves.

In seeking to comprehend the range of social relationships, we believe it also useful to think in terms of various analytical variables or dimensions upon which any relationship can be located for comparative purposes. One such dimension, important to all five papers, is *intimacy,* the breadth and depth of self-involvement of members in the relationship. A second is *duration,* whether measured in terms of calendar time or number of encounters. A third, which has received considerable attention here, is *formality,* the degree to which the social relationship is structured by some role relationship between the members. Fourth, and somewhat related to the third, is the dimension of *embeddedness* within some larger type of organization, such as family, school, or factory. A fifth dimension is the *actuality* of a relationship, the degree of manifestation in concrete encounters, as opposed to its remaining only on a symbolic plane. Sixth is *reciprocality,* the degree to which *both* members symbolize the existence of substantial probability of recurring interaction between them. A seventh dimension is *differentiation,* the degree to which members are distinguished from one another within such internal structures as power, status, affect, etc. These seven do not, of course, begin to exhaust pertinent dimensions for comparing social relationships, but they are surely among the more important.

It would obviously be possible to generate from these dimensions various typologies and taxonomies of relationships, but we feel that to do so would be premature. None of these dimensions is well conceptualized or measured, nor do we know much about how any two dimensions are empirically related. For example, although it might appear that intimacy and formality would be negatively related, Suttles has described important counter examples of formal relationships with considerable intimacy. We feel it is more appropriate at this point to seek to discover, over a wide range of content of relationships, the empirical relations among the various dimensions. Such knowledge would permit more reasonable construction of typologies and taxonomies in the future.

We are concerned that sociological analyses and studies of social relationships—including our own works to be sure—have thus far focused on one small though important segment of the total spectrum of social relationships. This segment consists of highly intimate, relatively enduring, and relatively voluntary relationships. We have many sociological works on friendship, courtship, and marriage; we have few on relationships between law partners, customers and clerks, mailmen and householders, secretaries and bosses, as *social* rather than *role* relationships. Do such social relationships resemble in structure, process, and function the sorts we have endeavored to analyze? Surely there are important variations.

RELATIONSHIPS AS SOCIAL ORGANIZATIONS

All five of our papers explicitly maintain that social relationships are a type of social organization. In this connection two points are particularly emphasized. First, the members, as well as certain outsiders, collectively recognize and symbolize the existence of the relationship as a social unit to which the members belong. Second, the members collectively evolve a private culture unique to the particular relationship (best seen in the more intimate, more enduring, more personal relationships on which we have focused here).

While G. McCall has provided a broad sketch of the emergent culture of a relationship, the others have examined particular features more closely. M. McCall has detailed how the goals or interests (focus) of a relationship give rise to a set of norms to maintain and effectuate this focus. Both Denzin and Suttles have analyzed the emergent rules of moral conduct within intimate relationships. Kurth has examined the differing obligations and sentiments in two types of relationships.

The matter of obligations and sentiments relates closely to the *social bonds* linking two persons in a relationship, also touched upon by G. McCall and Suttles. M. McCall's analysis of the focus and boundary rules of relationships deals with the *shape* of a relationship, a subject also discussed by G. McCall. The latter paper takes up as well the internal *social structure* of relationships; the discussion there of the power structure is amplified in the paper by Kurth.

Suttles examines friendships as a social *institution*, and certain institutionalized components are elaborated upon by Kurth, M. McCall, and Denzin.

THE ROLE OF DEVIANCE

Perhaps the most unexpected convergence is the insight by Denzin and Suttles that the culture, or moral order, of the intimate relationship stands in opposition to the societal rules of civil propriety. Not only are persons *allowed* to violate civil proprieties in an intimate relationship, but they are *required* to do so to affirm the private culture of the relationship. Moreover, Suttles shows that such signaling of one's membership in an intimate relationship is heightened by the fact that the normative order of the relationship is a quite simple and obvious transformation of the code of civil propriety.

In somewhat less dramatic ways, Kurth also discusses the role of deviation from the societal code.

Organizational Dynamics

The topic of organizational functioning, the carrying on of everyday collective business, is the least examined and most poorly understood aspect of social relationships. Just what do people do, and how, in order to be (rather than become) friends, lovers, co-workers, or legal adversaries? How do relationships, as social organizations, run?

Suttles poses this question sharply in the case of friendships. G. McCall examines sketchily some peculiarities in social relationships of certain common organizational processes—recruitment, socialization, interaction, innovation, social control, and logistics. Denzin considerably elaborates the discussion of social control, and Kurth describes certain features of ongoing exchange within established relationships.

Despite these beginnings, we feel that we, as well as others, have contributed only a little to understanding ordinary social process in relationships.

Organizational Change

Although we have had little to say concerning ordinary organizational process in relationships, we have put forward several thoughts on processes of change. They tend to fall under three major headings: the formation of relationships; the developmental sequence of relationships; and the transformation of relationships.

FORMATION OF RELATIONSHIPS

Among these three topics, we have had least to say concerning the formation of social relationships. G. McCall suggests that this process be viewed as organizational recruitment and points out certain distinguishing peculiarities of such recruitment in dyadic relationships.

Beyond this generic suggestion, the remaining contributions are concerned with the formation of one specific variety of relationship, viz., friendships. As Suttles points out, the one aspect of friendship that has been widely studied is the range of factors which promote interpersonal attraction and friendship formation. Accordingly, both papers on friendship in this volume have instead focused on factors that *inhibit* the formation of friendships. Kurth deals with informational barriers against adequate sampling of interpersonal rewards and costs, with organizational constraints against friendships, and with normative constraints on association across categories of age, sex, and marital status. Suttles likewise discusses organizational constraints and normative restrictions on association across class and ethnic boundaries.

On the positive side of friendship formation, both Kurth and Suttles examine key interpersonal *tactics* in the actual process of forming friendships, rather than disposing background factors. Kurth discusses the central role of interpersonal "moves" toward friendship, while Suttles emphasizes the similar signalizing (or recruitment) function of violations of public propriety that reveal one's "real self."

THE DEVELOPMENTAL SEQUENCE IN RELATIONSHIPS

Perhaps because all the papers are primarily concerned with rather intimate, relatively enduring, and relatively voluntary relationships, we tend to speak of a typical developmental sequence within relationships toward increased cohesiveness, elaboration, and intimacy.

Suttles, for example, establishes certain *gradients* of intimacy. This emphasis on changing activities is sustained by M. McCall, who locates the relevant dynamic in a chronic dissatisfaction with the boundary rules of relationships. G. McCall treats a similar dynamic of a "strain toward totality" in relationships and enumerates several factors serving to proliferate and to strengthen five types of social bonds uniting the members of a relationship. The latter thrust is further developed by Kurth in her exposition of various mechanisms, norms, and third-party dynamics that facilitate a progressive development toward friendship.

Although we have identified powerful, built-in strains toward such progressive development of at least these types of relationship, we have each denied that the developmental sequence is an inexorable one. Kurth has perhaps most clearly indicated why, and how, individuals often fight against and frequently overcome this strain toward greater involvement. It remains true, however, as Suttles puts it, that we have no studies of "friendship separation" comparable to the many studies of marital separation.

TRANSFORMATION OF RELATIONSHIPS

The transformation of social relationships, or of the basis for association, is here viewed as a quite normal and rather frequent process of change. M. McCall, for instance, views enduring relationships as passing through an endless sequence of *phases,* each marked off by an alteration of the boundary rules to include some new joint activity or to exclude some old one. G. McCall conceives of relationships as being in a continuous process of organizational change in which the interpersonal bonds, social structures, and the shape and culture of the relationship are constantly recast by external forces and by the internal organizational dynamics. Kurth views testing, expanding, and contracting relationships as normal features of negotiation within relationships.

In terms of more specific transformations, both papers on friendship treat friendship formation as a transformation of a relationship from some other basis. Kurth analyzes the possible transition from a friendly relation to friendship as taking place through social exchange calculations and symbolic interpersonal "moves." Suttles describes the transformation of a civil relationship into a friendship as taking place in good part through violations of public propriety.

Interorganizational Relations

No social organization can be fully understood viewed in isolation from its surrounding and interlinking organizations. This maxim is nowhere more true than in the case of social relationships. Because relationships are such small, emergent, and relatively resource-poor organizations, they tend to be embedded in or rather vulnerable to larger, more powerful, and more institutionalized organizations such as families, factories, and voluntary associations. On the other hand, social relationships may command greater allegiance and support from members, owing to the instrinsic sentimentalism and very personal rewards of such relationships.

Organizations may compete, conflict, or cooperate with one another, latently or manifestly. The process by which organizations (or individuals) balance and adjudicate the demands made by and upon them or their members is briefly discussed as one of *logistics* in the paper by G. McCall.

Very little is known of the interorganizational relations of social relationships. Our papers touch upon a few aspects of this problem largely to raise rather than answer questions.

COMMENSURATE ORGANIZATIONS

Any individual is involved in a number of social relationships at any one time. A central question is how the set of relationships so defined manage their mutual relations. M. McCall points out the stresses arising from the frequent sense of uniqueness and strain toward totality in any one relationship, which require its boundary rules to render other relationships relatively irrelevant. To the extent that the individual nevertheless obtains relevant rewards from other relationships, he tends to become alienated from the focal relationship.

Kurth emphasizes the role of other relationships in monitoring and enforcing commitments and the justice of bargaining within the focal relationship. Interlocking networks of relationships are seen as inhibiting the development of intimacy within any one of them. More broadly, the formation or development of any one relationship is greatly affected by the individuals' weight of existing commitments to other relationships.

LARGER ORGANIZATIONS

Suttles and Kurth examine how larger organizations both facilitate and inhibit the formation and development of social relationships between their members. That is, such organizations bring individuals into repeated contact and provide them with a formal relationship that might serve as the nucleus for the development of a more personal relationship. On the other hand, normative barriers are erected against such a development wherever the formal relationship is notably differentiated in terms of status or power, in order to prevent possible subversion of the division of labor in the larger organization.

Studies of primary groups in such organizations suggest, however, that the effects of emergent substructures may reinforce rather than subvert the larger division of labor, depending on the degree of consonance between the interests of the substructure and of the larger organization. Similar effects are surely characteristic of social relationships as well and are deserving of study.

Denzin, for example, shows that social relationships tend to relieve social control agencies of the difficulty of managing the bulk of deviant behavior and assist such agencies in their duties when a member's deviance becomes too great for relationships to manage.

"SMALLER" ORGANIZATIONS

Although no form of social organization can be literally smaller than a social relationship with only two members, there is a sense in which it is convenient to regard interactive encounters, which most often have only two members and are always much more transient than relationships, as being "smaller." In any case, we probably know more about the relation of social relationships to encounters than to any other type of organization.

M. McCall elucidates the structural basis for these close relations by showing the complementarity or reciprocality of focus and boundary rules between relationships and encounters. Dissatisfaction with the boundary rules of the encounter (dealing with identities) may lead to alienation from the focus of the relationship or vice versa.

The focal activity of an encounter between two persons impinges upon the boundary rules of their relationship and may thereby initiate a new phase in the relationship or reinforce the old one by providing fresh quantities of role support. Conversely, the existence of a social relationship profoundly sharpens and enriches interaction within the encounter by underlining its boundary rules. Kurth elaborates this point in showing that the demand for exchange parity within the encounter may thus be relaxed. Denzin and Suttles similarly show that conventional rules of propriety in encounters between relationship members are also relaxed or, more accurately, transformed to impart more intimacy to the interaction.

Functions and Dysfunctions for Individual and Society

INDIVIDUAL

As have other writers, we tend to emphasize the rewards obtained by the individual through membership in social relationships. Primary among these is support for personal identities, although many others can be enumerated, such as sex, status, power, com-panionship, material goods, and the like. As a counter theme, however, we have tried to bring out equally the corresponding costs involved in maintaining relationships.

For example, one important payoff of social relationships is the aid or favors received from the other member, such as a friend helping to paint the garage on the weekend or making a gift of his electric fan when he acquires an air conditioner. But the other side of a favor received is an obligation to return some favor later. In many cases the felt weight of the unspecified obligations of a relationship seem to outweigh the value of any particular favor one is likely to receive.

More closely related to the central focus on identities is the benefit of social insulation for one's deviance, failure, or attempts at personal growth by trying out new identities. The mutual ties and felt responsibility within a relationship allow one to depart from the model of decorum and competence without incurring major sanctions. At the same time, however, he does make known these departures to his relationship partner and thus risks exposure should the relationship sour, departures become too great, or the partner irresponsibly pass on knowledge of these departures.

In sum, we have attempted to redress the balance in our pictures of relationships. While most social relationships do make life more rewarding and humanely comfortable for individuals, even primary relationships are costly, demanding, and hazardous. Accordingly, we have sought to portray the deep ambivalence and devastating potential for interpersonal conflict that characterize such idealized relationships as marriage and friendship.

SOCIETY

We earlier touched upon certain broad social functions of relationships, including the insulation of deviance and the reinforcement or subversion of institutional functioning.

An additional social consequence of relationships is their tendency to evade norms and institutionalized practices while pursuing established goals. The larger division of labor may be contravened in favor of some situationally emergent division that perhaps gets the job done more efficiently under the immediate circumstances.

The close understanding and mutual commitments of relationship members enable them to improvise what Weber would call substantively rational solutions. This improvisation is achieved, however, at the expense of formal rationality, the formally established division of labor. Once contravened, formal rationality may be difficult to re-establish, as the mystique of status and power has been pierced by personal relationships. The effectiveness of formal rationality stems from its applicability independent of particular personnel, whereas emergent solutions depend on the particular relationships that have developed. Any turnover in personnel therefore renders substantive rationality tenuous. Further, emergent solutions based upon personal relationships may be a serious obstacle to implementing any changes in formal operating procedures.

One further social function of relationships discussed here is the "bridging function" of friendships, serving partially to integrate disparate sectors of society. While this function is not to be gainsaid, the particularizing consequences of relationships may equally give rise to a kind of separatism or provincialism, in which members support one another's withdrawal from or ignoring of societal norms and values.

The societal import of social relationships, we must conclude, has been little explored in any serious way.

Problems of Research

In the course of this overview we have remarked upon the relative absence of research on a large number of questions. In closing, we should like to comment upon what seem to be important factors contributing to the paucity of studies of relationships.

One such factor has been the absence of a proper conceptual framework for posing and relating relevant questions. Most recent research on interpersonal phenomena has been framed in terms of role theory, interpersonal theory, or balance theory, ignoring the traditional sociological concern with social organization. We are hopeful that the ideas presented in this volume may be useful in generating more appropriate lines of research on social relationships.

A second factor has been the lack of a sampling frame for social relationships. We cannot of course provide such a frame here, but we hope that our discussions of the range of social relationships may contribute to this end. Students of particular varieties of relationships, such as courtship, marriage, and friendship, have attained reasonable success in sampling relationships, a fact that bodes well for the study of other varieties.

Third, many of the most neglected aspects of the study of social relationships—e.g., their dynamics and processes of change—additionally require laborious and expensive longitudinal research designs. We can say only that we feel the returns would surely repay the investment.

Finally, certain organizational features of relationships themselves serve to impede their study. For example, the intimacy and sentimentalism of relationships disposes the members to shield them from objective analysis. Also, the close presence of an observer effectively converts the relationship into a triad, whose instability and peculiar dynamics were well remarked by Georg Simmel. Further, the tendency of members to see only the other person and not an overarching social organization (a feature also noted by Simmel) makes it more difficult to gather data on social relationships even by interviews.

Surely none of these obstacles to research on social relationships will prove insuperable. Participant observation of relationships in which the observer is a *bona fide* member, unobtrusive observation (as by telemetry), theoretically informed repeated interviews, and laboratory observation of experimentally created relationships ought, in various combinations, to allow sociologists to gain much greater scientific understanding of social relationships.

Bibliography

Argyle, Michael
   1967 The Psychology of Interpersonal Behavior. Baltimore: Penguin.

Becker, Howard S.
   1960 "Notes on the concept of commitment." American Journal of Sociology, 66:32–40.
   1963 Outsiders: Studies in the Sociology of Deviance. New York: Free Press.
Bittner, Egon
   1967a "The police on skid-row: a study of peace keeping." American Sociological Review, 32:699–715.
   1967b "Police discretion in apprehending the mentally ill." Social Problems, 14:278–292.
Bond, John R. and W. Edgar Vinacke
   1961 "Coalitions in mixed sex triads." Sociometry, 24:61–75.
Brim, Orville G., Jr.
   1966 "Socialization through the life-cycle." In Orville G. Brim, Jr. and Stanton Wheeler, Socialization After Childhood. New York: Wiley. Pp. 1–49.
Bucher, Rue and Anselm Strauss
   1961 "Professions in process." American Journal of Sociology, 66:325–334.
Buck, Vernon E.
   1966 "A model for viewing an organization as a system of constraints." In James D. Thompson, ed., Approaches to Organizational Design. Pittsburgh: University of Pittsburgh Press. Pp. 103–172.
Burgess, Ernest W. and Paul Wallin
   1943 "Homogamy in social characteristics." American Journal of Sociology, 49:109–124.

183

Cartwright, Dorwin and Frank Harary
  1956   "Structural balance: a generalization of Heider's theory."
  Psychological Review, 63:277–293.
Cicourel, Aaron V.
  1968   The Social Organization of Juvenile Justice. New York:
  Wiley.
Cobb, Humphrey
  1935   Paths of Glory. New York: Viking Press.
Cooley, Charles Horton
  1902   Human Nature and the Social Order. New York: Scribner's.
  1909   Social Organization. New York: Scribner's.
  1956   Social Organization. New York: Free Press.
Coser, Lewis
  1964   "The political functions of eunuchism." American Sociological
  Review, 29:880–885.
Cumulative Index to the American Journal of Sociology
  1966   Chicago: University of Chicago Press.

Dalton, Melville
  1959   Men Who Manage. New York: Wiley.
Davis, Fred
  1961   "Deviance disavowal: the management of strained interaction by the visibly handicapped." Social Problems, 9:120–132.
Denzin, Norman K.
  1969   "Symbolic interactionism and ethnomethodology: a proposed
  synthesis." American Sociological Review, 34:922–934.
Douglas, Jack D.
  1970   Deviance and Respectability: The Social Construction of
  Moral Meanings. New York: Basic Books.

Edgerton, Robert
  1967   The Cloak of Competence. Berkeley: University of California
  Press.
Emerson, Richard M.
  1962   "Power-dependence relations." American Sociological Review, 27:31–41.

Farber, Bernard
  1964   Family: Organization and Interaction. San Francisco:
  Chandler.
  1968   Mental Retardation: Its Social Context and Social Consequences. Boston: Houghton Mifflin.
Festinger, Leon, Stanley Schachter and Kurt W. Back
  1959   Social Pressures in Informal Groups. New York: Harper.

Firth, Raymond
1936 "Bond friendship." In I.H. Dudley, ed., Custom is King: Essays Presented to R.R. Marett on his 70th Birthday. London: Buxton.

Gans, Herbert J.
1962 Urban Villagers. New York: Free Press.
Garfinkel, Harold
1967 Studies in Ethnomethodology. Englewood Cliffs, N.J.: Prentice-Hall.
Geertz, Clifford
1963 Old Societies and New States. New York: Free Press.
Glaser, Daniel
1964 The Effectiveness of a Prison and Parole System. Indianapolis: Bobbs-Merrill.
Goffman, Erving
1959 Presentation of Self in Everyday Life. New York: Doubleday.
1961a Asylums. New York: Doubleday.
1961b Encounters. Indianapolis: Bobbs-Merrill.
1963a Behavior in Public Places. New York: Free Press.
1963b Stigma. Englewood Cliffs, N.J.: Prentice-Hall.
1967 Interaction Ritual. New York: Doubleday.
Goode, William J.
1960 "A theory of role strain." American Sociological Review, 25:483–496.
Gouldner, Alvin W.
1959 "Organizational analysis." In Robert K. Merton, Leonard Broom and Leonard S. Cottrell, Jr., eds., Sociology Today. New York: Basic Books.
1960 "The norm of reciprocity: a preliminary statement." American Sociological Review, 25:161–178.
Gross, Edward and Gregory P. Stone
1963 "Embarrassment and the analysis of role requirements." American Journal of Sociology, 70:1–15.
Gullahorn, J.T.
1952 "Distance and friendship as factors in the gross interaction matrix." Sociometry, 15:123–134.

Heggen, Thomas
1946 Mr. Roberts. New York: Houghton Mifflin.
Heider, Fritz
1958 The Psychology of Interpersonal Relations: New York: Wiley.
Hodge, Robert W., Paul M. Siegel and Peter H. Rossi
1964 "Occupational prestige in the United States: 1925–1963." American Journal of Sociology, 70:286–302.

Hollander, E.P.
1958 "Conformity, status and idiosyncracy credit." Psychological Review, 65:117–127.
Hollingshead, August B. and Frederick C. Redlich
1958 Social Class and Mental Illness. New York: Wiley.
Homans, George C.
1950 The Human Group. New York: Harcourt Brace.
1954 "The cash posters." American Sociological Review, 19:724–733.
1961 Social Behavior: Its Elementary Forms. New York: Harcourt Brace.
Hsi Men
1960 Ching Pei Mei (The Gold Lotus). New York: Capricorn Books.
Hughes, Everett C.
1945 "Dilemmas and contradictions of status." American Journal of Sociology, 50:353–359.

Icheiser, Gustav
1949 Misunderstandings in Human Relationships: A Study in False Social Perceptions. Chicago: University of Chicago Press.
Index to the American Sociological Review
1961 New York: American Sociological Association.

Jackson, Joan
1962 "Alcoholism and the family." In David J. Pittman and Charles R. Snyder, eds., Society, Culture and Personality. New York: Wiley. Pp. 472–492.
Jones, Edward E. and Keith E. Davis
1965 "From acts to dispositions: the attribution process in person perception." In Leonard Berkowitz, ed., Advances in Experimental Social Psychology, Vol. II. New York: Academic Press. Pp. 219–266.
Jourard, Sidney M.
1964 The Transparent Self. Princeton: Van Nostrand.
Kantrowitz, Nathan
Joliet Terms. Unpublished manuscript.
Kesey, Ken
1962 One Flew over the Cookoo's Nest. New York: Viking Press.
Keil, Charles
1966 Urban Blues. Chicago: University of Chicago Press.
Kitsuse, John I. and Aaron V. Cicourel
1963 "A note on the uses of official statistics." Social Problems, 11:131–139.
Landers, Ann
1952 Dating's Do's and Don'ts. Chicago: Field Enterprises.

Landesco, John
1964 "Organized crime in Chicago." In Ernest W. Burgess and Donald J. Bogue, eds., Contributions to Urban Sociology. Chicago: University of Chicago Press. Pp. 559–576.

Landy, David and Sara E. Singer
1961 "The social organization of a club for former mental patients." Human Relations, 14:31–41.

Lazarsfeld, Paul F. and Robert K. Merton
1954 "Friendship as a social process." In Morroe Berger, Theodore Abel and Charles H. Page, eds., Freedom and Control in Modern Society. Princeton: Van Nostrand. Pp. 18–66.

Levi-Strauss, Claude
1966 The Savage Mind. Chicago: University of Chicago Press.

Lindzey, Gardner and Edgar F. Borgatta
1954 "Sociometric measurement." In Gardner Lindzey, ed., Handbook of Social Psychology, Vol. I. Cambridge, Mass.: Addison-Wesley. Pp. 405–448.

Little, Roger W.
1964 "Buddy relations and combat performance." In Morris Janowitz, ed., The New Military. New York: Russell Sage Foundation. Pp. 195–224.

Lofland, John
1968 "The youth ghetto." Journal of Higher Education, 29:121–143.
1969 Deviance and Identity. Englewood Cliffs, N.J.: Prentice-Hall.

McCall, George J. and J.L. Simmons
1966 Identities and Interactions. New York: Free Press.

Marquand, John P.
1952 Point of No Return. New York: Random House.

Matza, David
1964 Delinquency and Drift. New York: Wiley.

Maurer, David W.
1962 The Big Con. New York: Signet.

Miller, Walter B.
1958 "Lower class culture as a generating milieu of gang delinquency." Journal of Social Issues, 14(3):5–19.

Mullahy, Patrick
1949 A Study of Interpersonal Relations. New York: Hermitage.

Nadel, S.F.
1957 The Theory of Social Structure. New York: Free Press.

Newcomb, Theodore M.
1956 "The prediction of interpersonal attraction." American Psy-

chologist, 11:575–586.
1961   The Acquaintance Process. New York: Holt Rinehart & Winston.

Ohlin, Lloyd, Herman Piven and Donnell Pappenfort
1956   "Major dilemmas of the social worker in probation and parole." National Probation and Parole Association Journal, 2:211–225.
Orwell, George
1953   Such, Such, Were the Joys. New York: Harcourt Brace.

Parsons, Talcott
1951   The Social System. New York: Free Press.
1959   "The professions and social structure." Social Forces, 17:457–467.

Rainwater, Lee
1966   "The problem of lower class culture." Paper prepared for the Department of Sociology Colloquium, University of Wisconsin, September 23, 1966.
Roth, Julius
1963   Timetables. Indianapolis: Bobbs-Merrill.
Roy, Donald
1960   "Banana time." Human Organization, 18:158–168.

Sampson, Harold, Sheldon L. Messinger and Robert D. Towne
1962   "Family processes and becoming a mental patient." American Journal of Sociology, 62:88–96.
Scheff, Thomas J.
1963   "The role of the mentally ill and the dynamics of mental illness." Sociometry, 26:436–453.
Schorr, Alvin L.
1963   Slums and Social Insecurity. Report No. 1. Washington, D.C.: Social Security Administration, Division of Research and Statistics.
Schutz, William A.
1967   Joy, Expanding Human Awareness. New York: Grove Press.
Scott, W. Richard
1964   "Theory of organizations." In Robert E.L. Faris, ed., Handbook of Modern Sociology. Chicago: Rand McNally. Pp. 492–495.
Secord, Paul F. and Carl W. Backman
1964   Social Psychology. New York: McGraw-Hill.
Service, Elman R.
1962   Primital Social Organization. New York: Random House.

Shibutani, Tamotsu
1962 "Reference groups and social control." In Arnold M. Rose, ed., Human Behavior and Social Processes. Boston: Houghton Mifflin. Pp. 129–147.

Shils, Edward A.
1957 "Primordial, personal, sacred and civil ties." British Journal of Sociology, 8:130–145.

Shils, Edward A. and Morris Janowitz
1948 "Cohesion and disintegration in the Wehrmacht in World War II." Public Opinion Quarterly, 12:280–315.

Simmel, Georg
1950 The Sociology of Georg Simmel. Kurt Wolff, tr. New York: Free Press.

Simmons, Ozzie G., James A. Davis and Katherine Spencer
1956 "Interpersonal strains in release from a mental hospital." Social Problems, 4:21–28.

Simon, Rita James
1967 The Jury and the Defense of Sanity. Boston: Little, Brown.

Singer, Milton
1960 "Contra-culture and subculture." American Sociological Review, 25:625–635.

Spitzer, Stephan and Norman K. Denzin
1968 The Mental Patient: Studies in the Sociology of Deviance. New York: McGraw-Hill.

Stone, Gregory P.
1962 "Appearance and the self." In Arnold M. Rose, ed., Human Behavior and Social Processes. Boston: Houghton Hifflin. Pp. 86–118.

Strauss, Anselm
1959 Mirrors and Masks. New York: Free Press.

Sullivan, Harry Stack
1964 The Collected Works of Harry Stack Sullivan (2 Vols.). New York: Norton.

Suttles, Gerald D.
1968 The Social Order of the Slum. Chicago: University of Chicago Press.

Sykes, Gresham
1958 Society of Captives. Princeton: University of Princeton Press.

Szasz, Thomas S.
1963 Law, Liberty and Psychiatry. New York: Macmillan.

Thibaut, John W. and Harold H. Kelley
1959 The Social Psychology of Groups. New York: Wiley.

Thompson, Hunter S.
1966 Hell's Angels. New York: Random House.

Thrasher, Frederick M.
1963   The Gang (abridged edition). Chicago: University of Chicago Press.
Toby, Jackson
1952   "Some variables in role conflict analysis." Social Forces, 30:323–327.
Tomeh, Aida K.
1962   "Informal participation in a metropolitan community." Sociological Quarterly, 8:85–102.

Vinacke, W. Edgar
1959   "Sex roles in a three-person game." Sociometry, 22:343–369.
Vold, George
1958   Theoretical Criminology. New York: Oxford University Press.

Waller, Willard
1937   "The rating and dating complex." American Sociological Review, 2:727–734.
1938   The Family: A Dynamic Interpretation. New York: Dryden.
Weber, Max
1947   The Theory of Social and Economic Organization. A.M. Henderson and Talcott Parsons, tr. New York: Free Press.
Webster's New World Dictionary
1955   New York: World.
Weinstein, Eugene A., William L. DeVaughn and Mary Glenn Wiley
1969   "Obligations and the flow of deference in exchange." Sociometry, 32:1–12.
Wentworth, Harold and Stuart Berg Flexner
1960   Dictionary of American Slang. New York: Crowell.
Wood, Margaret M.
1934   The Stranger: A Study in Social Relationships. New York: Columbia University Press.

Analytical Index

A Selective Page Guide to Important Themes

THE NATURE OF SOCIAL RELATIONSHIPS, 171–174

Definition of Social Relationship, 171–172
Interpersonal emphasis, 4–6, 41–42, 67–68, 98–100, 136
Emphasis on probability of recurring interaction, 4, 8, 10, 42, 66–68, 131–132, 163
Members' symbolization of relationship, 4, 18–19, 41, 66–70, 98–100, 152–157
Fit between members' roles or selves, 10–12, 41, 69–70, 98–100, 136–137

The Range of Social Relationships, 172–173
Differentiation dimension, 12–15, 120–126, 147
Formality dimension, 4–5, 41–42, 100–103, 136, 138
Intimacy dimension, 9, 44–45, 66, 70, 128–132, 136–137, 140–141
Other dimensions, 19–20, 66–71, 97, 99–100, 138–142

Relationships as Social Organizations, 173–174
Affirmation of organizational view, 16–17, 41, 73, 95–98, 138–142
collective symbolization of relationships, 18–19, 43, 73, 98–100, 152–157
culture of relationships, 15–16, 41–45, 71–78, 116–120, 141–142, 161–162

191